About Talking to Babies

In recent years, scientific research has significantly advanced our knowledge of the human brain's capacity to process complex information even during the prenatal and early postnatal period. It is also evident that newborn babies respond to their parents' emotional lives, although it is not well understood how they do so. Dr. Myriam Szejer, a French psychoanalyst, adds another dimension to this growing body of knowledge. In more than a decade of work with patients at the Antoine Béclère maternity ward in Paris, Dr. Szejer and her colleagues have developed ways of intervening with newborns who are in acute distress with no apparent medical reason for their problems. By connecting these often severe symptoms of intense crying and feeding, sleeping, digestive problems, etc. with painful losses (often perinatal) and other traumatic events in their families that took place before they were born, Dr. Szejer has created "conversations" with these young infants. Often in the presence of their parents, she interprets—puts into words—for them the meaning of their symptoms, encourages them to live, and frees them and their birth or adoptive parents to embark on a positive life together. As I read Dr. Szejer's account of this work in her book, *Talking to Babies,* I wondered if these skills could be taught to others who are working with infants and their families, and if this model of intervention could be replicated in places like the United States, where the average stay in a maternity hospital is only half the usual four-day period in France. I certainly hope so. In any case, Dr. Szejer and her staff offer a precious gift to their patient population at the Béclère maternity ward.

CATHERINE BUTTENWIESER
early childhood social worker,
Children's Hospital, Boston

It is hard to believe, perhaps, that a very young, ailing baby can actually find relief when a correct explanation of her misery is given to her in her mother's presence, and yet Myriam Szejer makes the case over and over again in *Talking to Babies*. Words that reveal a hidden truth carry an emotional charge that can heal trauma even in premature babies. As the data accumulated in this interesting book aptly suggest, we may be closer to understanding how the invisible cord that connects the infant's body to his mother's psyche is made up of unspoken experiences and memories that can only be made clear through the power of interpretation.

Talking to Babies shows that psychoanalytic research not only confirms the recent discoveries of neurolinguistics and developmental psychology but also offers new guidelines for further exploration of the complex relation between infants and their mothers. Thanks to works like this, scientists may become less resistant to the idea that the mind, the body, and the other are connected through unconscious processes that are both shaped and revealed by strings of words. Myriam Szejer sets the stage for a new field that would bring under the same roof the life of neurons, hormones, and family history.

JUDITH FEHER-GUREWICH
coeditor of The Subject and the Self

Talking to Babies marks a new moment in the development of psychoanalytic theory and practice. Dr. Szejer is a master analyst who uses her craft as first aid for infants and parents in crisis. Her book distills psychoanalytic principles and demonstrates their practical value for understanding the emotional intensities surrounding birth. *Talking to Babies* has a great deal to teach about using language to give infants the dignity and respect they need to flourish. Both medical professionals and general readers will gain a deep appreciation of the profound impact of words in the earliest days of every human life.

NAOMI GOLDENBERG
author of Returning Words to Flesh:
Feminism, Psychoanalysis, and
the Resurrection of the Body

Talking to Babies

Healing with Words on a Maternity Ward

MYRIAM SZEJER, M.D.

With the collaboration of Hervé Bernard
Translated from the French by Jane Marie Todd

Beacon Press, Boston

BEACON PRESS
25 Beacon Street, Boston, Massachusetts 02108-2892
www.beacon.org

Beacon Press books
are published under the auspices of
the Unitarian Universalist Association of Congregations.

09 08 07 06 05   8 7 6 5 4 3 2 1

This book is printed on acid-free paper that meets the uncoated paper
ANSI/NISO specifications for permanence as revised in 1992.

Text design by Isaac Tobin
Composition by Wilsted & Taylor Publishing Services

LIBRARY OF CONGRESS CATALOGING-IN-PUBLICATION DATA
Szejer, Myriam.
    [Des mots pour naître. English]
    Talking to babies : healing with words on a maternity ward / Myriam Szejer; with
the collaboration of Hervé Bernard; translated from the French by Jane Marie Todd.
        p. cm.
    Translation of: Des mots pour naître. Paris : Gallimard, c. 1997.
    ISBN 0-8070-2114-8 (cloth : alk. paper)
    1. Infant psychiatry. 2. Infants (Newborn)—Psychology. 3. Interpersonal
communication in infants. 4. Psychoanalysis. I. Bernard, Hervé. II. Title.
    RJ502.5.S9813 2004
    618.92′89—dc22

                                                                        2003014846

This work was published with generous assistance from the French Ministry of
Culture—National Book Center.

Ouvrage publié avec le concours du Ministère française chargé de la culture—
Centre national de livre.

© Editions GALLIMARD, Paris, 1997

To all babies,
newborns past and newborns present

To François

Contents

Preface

Sometimes, as I am leaving the hospital late at night, I stop on the way to look in on a patient who has recently given birth. And often, as I open the door, I catch a special moment: the new mother leaning over the crib, or more often face to face with the newborn on her lap, looking intently at him and murmuring motherly words. The striking thing is the mixture of intensity and gentleness, the timbre and tone of her voice, the depth of her gaze.

In a maternity ward, however, everything is not always so rosy. Sometimes the mother is not in awe; sometimes her words are inappropriate or slow in coming—or worse, missing.

Yes, birth is sometimes accompanied by suffering, a suffering too rarely perceived in our Western societies, where we think only of the fantastic progress obstetrics has made in improving the conditions for giving birth, both for the mother and for the newborn. If we pay attention, however, we may discover painful relationships or secret tragedies that will later generate suffering, violence, mistreatment.

The obstetrician is in the delivery business, interested

primarily in the women, the mothers, but he cannot neglect to take an interest in the baby's journey. When I met Myriam Szejer, an unknown field opened to me: the reality of the newborn's preverbal behavior. Of course, we should pay attention to our own interpretations, our projections; but Myriam Szejer has opened new avenues. She dares psychoanalyze newborns, dares talk to them, dares intervene before the symptom has taken root, particularly in dangerous situations. Her approach ought to become known to all who make perinatal medicine their career. Her approach is innovative; her interpretations ought to be further elaborated upon. What woman has not been shaken to her very being by becoming a mother; what man has not trembled at becoming a father? Babies feel that profound or passing apprehensiveness. They need to be listened to, which is a form of respect.

RENÉ FRYDMAN, M.D.

René Frydman is head of the
Department of Gynecology and Obstetrics
at Antoine Béclère Hospital in Paris.

Introduction

"WE HEREBY ANNOUNCE ..."

"There is an age when you teach what you know; but then you reach an age when you teach what you do not know: this is called seeking." —ROLAND BARTHES

There are days in this profession when you feel very little. Whatever pride you take in your experience as a psychoanalyst, in your years as a psychiatrist to adults and children, in the lessons your teachers have taught you, it is no use. When a patient tells you that all the world's misery has fallen on her shoulders, you have nothing to say. In fact, however, this is of little consequence. Being quiet affords you the opportunity to hear. And, should the occasion later arise, to say something.

I had been going through this experience for some years when one morning, arriving at the maternity ward as I did every Monday, I sensed something strange happening on the postdelivery floor. Apparently, there was nothing seriously wrong, but the pediatricians, the midwives, the nurses for adult patients and for newborns all seemed oddly anxious about a new mother, Mrs. Lemercier. She had given birth two days earlier to her first child, a son, whom she had named Yvon. The delivery had gone very well, and she had been particularly happy since, three years earlier, she had lost the child she was carrying four months before term. There was just one minor detail, which had created that vague uneasiness in the staff: When she got back to her room, Mrs. Lemercier scrupulously turned out all the lights and pulled the curtains. Since that moment, she had lived shut up in the dark. Because she had no complaints and had made no comment about her behavior, no one knew what to think, and everyone refrained from questioning her. Everyone hoped that her peculiar actions would prove inconsequential. Nevertheless, members of the staff were perplexed. Although they were accustomed to pointing out to me mothers who might benefit from my services, they were reluctant to speak to me about the concern this one was causing them. Everyone seemed upset but the patient.

On Monday morning, however, there was a new reason for anxiety, this time in Mrs. Lemercier herself. She had been seized with panic at the thought that her baby, who was now two days old, "had not peed yet." She called in the pediatrician who, after having the child drink, examined him in front of his mother. Very quickly, during the exam itself, Yvon began to urinate, to the great relief of his mother, who was looking on. The pediatrician, however, believed that this was not the first time the child had urinated and that the urinary retention was a fantasy on the mother's part, the result of anxiety. With the agreement of the midwife, she decided to explain to Mrs. Lemercier that there was a "psychoanalyst for babies" at that hospital, and that she could meet with me if she wanted to talk about her concerns. Since Mrs. Lemercier had been extremely reticent until that time about what was happening to her, they were afraid she would refuse. But, to their great surprise, she agreed to see me.

In fact, she specifically wanted to speak to a psychoanalyst. I soon learned why. At one time, she had sought out the services of a psychiatrist; then, on the advice of her mother (who had asked the opinion of a psychiatrist of her acquaintance), she had entered psychoanalysis, where she remained for several years. With little hesitation, she now welcomed the idea of speaking to me in my capacity as a psychoanalyst.

The Sufferings of a Mother, of a Woman, of a Daughter

Scarcely had I entered the room and introduced myself when she spoke to me of her sufferings as a woman and as a mother. When she was twelve years old, shortly after her first menstrual period, she had begun to suffer from amenorrhea, interruption of menses, which had ended only when she met her husband-to-be at age eighteen. Several years later, she was again suffering. She and her husband wanted a child and had nearly lost hope that they would ever have one. When I asked her if anything unusual had happened when she was twelve, she related the following story. Her father, who was enormously respected by everyone, including herself, had asked her one day to fetch a bottle of wine. Happy to be given this honor and anxious to do well, she rushed down to the wine cellar, fell on her way back up the stairs, broke the selected bottle, and seriously injured her knee. A tendon was severed and she required surgery. Shortly after her operation, the Lemercier family took a trip to the beach. An excellent swimmer, so she said, she had gone out into the water. But then she had the sudden sensation that her injured knee was not responding, that her leg was paralyzed, and that she was going to drown. She called for help. Her father dived in, but he was knocked unconscious and pulled under the water. It was her turn to try to save him. She thought she had recovered the use of her knee, and made every effort to get him to shore, but he was a heavy man and it was beyond her ability. She again yelled for help, this time for her father. By the time the rescuers pulled the two of them out, he was already dead. It was that horrible event that the darkness of her hospital room seemed to be commemorating. Was she, without being conscious of it, completing her mourning for her father?

Let's look at this story, scene by scene.

In the first scene, the young girl, having gone to fetch a bottle at her father's request, falls and injures her knee. This simple action condenses the most varied elements of the family romance, and constitutes a veritable message in a bottle, which she would decipher much later, after Yvon's birth. In the second scene, the father dies. It is as if, for a long period of time, that extremely painful episode established the tragic character of the first moment, as if the second act in the drama revealed a posteriori the decisive importance of the first, rather than the reverse. Psychoanalysts are accustomed to such deferred effects. Two powerful scenes, two calls for help, just like, later on, two babies—and two psychoanalysts—established a connection between the articulation of this drama and the symbolic form it took. The third scene in this drama is the birth of the child and the mother's anxiety about his capacity to urinate. If I add that the paternal grandparents had a significant history of alcoholism, it will be clear that, from the broken bottle and spilt blood in the first act, the drowning and amenorrhea in the second, all the way to the reassuring urination produced by the baby in the third act—a lot of water (and blood) had passed under the bridge. Granted. The problem is that the water might have run dry. The amenorrhea dated from the father's drowning, and that amenorrhea seemed to serve the function of drying up the blood of the wound. The body failed to respond to the father's summons to fetch the wine; the body was silent in the face of the father's death, which it believed it had caused. Mrs. Lemercier's suffering upon the death of that beloved father was, so to speak, mute. She remained in a state of shock for two days after her father's death, and then she threw herself from the roof of the family home in front of a group of people. As a matter of fact, she had gone up on the roof to play, as she frequently did. Her family, given the context, became alarmed on seeing her up there. When they were unable to get her to come down, someone called the firefighters, who had just enough time to take their places before she jumped. Had she consciously attempted suicide? No one could say, not even she, since she totally erased those three days from her memory, and reconstituted the scene on the basis of what she was told during her analysis. She was an amnesiac, then, but she was not forgetful. She herself said how, as an adolescent, she would provoke her mother to slap her, with, in her head, a ready-made response: "You hit me because I killed Daddy!"

THE PLACE OF THE CHILD

In place of the mourning for her father, which she found impossible to perform, there was only guilt. The amenorrhea that followed attests to that. Furthermore, this post-traumatic symptom disappeared when she met her husband-to-be at age eighteen. Reconciled with the male figure, she regained a part of her femininity. But then she encountered infertility problems a few years later. She was a woman, yes, but not yet a mother. In fact, Yvon's birth was particularly welcome because it ended a long period of suffering associated with her efforts to bear a child. A few years earlier, Mrs. Lemercier had solicited the help of a gynecologist to treat her infertility. The treatments did not have the anticipated success, and she decided to end them. In the weeks following that decision, she became pregnant without medical intervention. That pregnancy ended in a miscarriage at twenty-three weeks. That first child, a stillbirth, was given the name Jean-Yves, which combined two names, one chosen by the father, the other by the mother. It would be echoed in the name of the second child, Yvon. A period of infertility lasting more than three years followed and persuaded Mrs. Lemercier to consult the Béclère Hospital, on the advice of a woman friend she respected. Apparently reassured by the idea of getting care at a hospital, she began a new infertility treatment. That treatment, which was, in fact, minor, very quickly resulted in another pregnancy. She was happy about that success and relieved at the idea of being cared for at Béclère. It was in that climate of trust that Yvon was born.

Perhaps the miscarriage had been connected to her guilt, as if it signified: I killed my father, the gods are hungry for revenge, they demand the child be sacrificed. In any case, to become a mother, she would have to go against the taboo associated with her unperformed mourning. In addition, she would have to be able to identify with her mother. To assume her maternal role, she had to come to terms with the only model of motherhood that matters for a woman who has just given birth—her own mother. As she told me during our interview, she had a high opinion of her mother, and that respect extended even to her professional life. Like her mother, Mrs. Lemercier worked in the world of medicine. It is also clear why it was on her mother's advice that she entered psychoanalysis. I believe these elements of maternal identification were not unrelated to her decision to be treated for infertility and to get her prenatal care specifically at a hospital. They explain in good part the reassurance she found there. It was at the hospital that she was able to become a mother, because it was at the hospital that she could be mothered.

There is no need to interpret this story at greater length, since the narration of this portion of it is already an interpretation, marked as it is by the work Mrs. Lemercier did in analysis over several years. By contrast, I am obliged by that narrative to point out the site where the child came to take his place. In this instance, the newborn came to the place where the mourning for the father could be performed; he may have been the one who would allow it to come to an end. He responded to it, beyond the mother's request, via urination. She told me, in fact, that she had the feeling her child began to live only after that "life-saving" pee; until then, she explained, he had felt only suffering and anxiety.

How better to represent matters than by saying: The child's urination, though it once more placed his mother in the situation where tragedy had left her, granted her access to a new destiny. The child's "deluge" thus gave a new meaning to the liquid, the water, the sea that had killed his grandfather. It was, we might say, the signifier of a new baptism. The round of deaths and births never ends, but for Mrs. Lemercier it stopped at the fact that the living can be an occasion for celebrating the dead. That was the meaning of the ritual set in place in the new mother's hospital room. In return, for this woman, whose relationship with an admirable father was so cruelly ended by his death, the tribute paid to a father, symbolically dead this time, was the occasion for a hopeful welcome to the living child. The child's "symptom" was like the grain of sand that derailed his mother's deadly logic and led them both to a new presence in the world.

FROM DEATH TO LIFE

That this "analysis baby" chose to live, unlike his elder brother, was in itself a living response to his grandfather's death. His birth steered the mother toward the meaning of symbolic debt through the mourning performed. For her, the symbolic father was the dead father. The real father, a mythical figure in Mrs. Lemercier's family, was himself the child of alcoholic and abusive parents. At the age of eighteen, he ran off to join the army. Later, he managed to be named his brother's guardian, and had him placed in an institution to protect him. Both eldest son and guardian, if not paterfamilias, he thereby made an important symbolic leap, and, in fact, not just a symbolic one. In the army, he had a growth spurt of eight inches in two years. On his own, he managed to provide for the needs of his entire family, and at thirty-eight he married a woman of eighteen.

To end this account of tragedy with a touch of comedy, let me make this final observation. This baby, in coming into the world, got his mother out of prison. Mrs. Lemercier, after getting civil service training, had found a job in the prison system, where her husband was already working. As it happened, during her second pregnancy, her husband was transferred. After her maternity leave, she returned to work, but outside the penitentiary system. That happy event coincided with Yvon's arrival.

A death announcement can, as in this case, be combined with a birth announcement. When we announce an event that affects us, we address society, even if it consists only of a limited group of friends or relatives, and we ask them, not simply to share our sorrow or joy, but to recognize it as admissible. An announcement assumes trust in the other, who is summoned to be a witness to that suffering or that joy, combined with a hope that that trust will allow us to move on. In that sense, we all need to bear witness to what makes up our life, to share with the other what belongs to us, in order to go forward. This is true within the framework of a psychoanalytic dialogue: Mrs. Lemercier was thus able to find an outlet for the things left unsaid that were reducing her to silence. It is also true within the perspective of a book like this one, which intends to be the record of an experiment. It is therefore time to give a full account of the genesis of that experiment.

The Three Moments of Psychoanalysis

"Psychoanalysts in the maternity ward are nothing new," said obstetrician René Frydman to a journalist who was questioning him about my work on his ward. "Psychoanalysts who talk to babies are." Let us state one thing clearly: There are no psychoanalysts for newborns, just as there are no psychoanalysts for adults or for children. That is simply a manner of speaking, which, in our profession, allows us to articulate differences we may have in terms of technique or experience. There are only psychoanalysts, period. We are psychoanalysts in the first place, prior to any reference to Freud and his successors, because subjects in their suffering call upon us to be psychoanalysts.

What is new in the matter is that we systematically, methodically, and patiently reach out to recognize the newborn's irreducible desire: first, because he was born for a reason; and second, because he may be stuck in symptoms that medicine cannot always explain, and, if so, there is a very good chance that his irreducible human desire has been thwarted. Nothing I am saying here is a theoretical wager. I have learned it from the newborns themselves.

For example, in the early days of my practice with babies, I saw a mother for an apparently harmless case of "baby blues." She was engaged in polite conversation with me, when, suddenly, the child, hearing me call him by his name and begin to repeat his story to him, began to move about and moan, despite the fact that his mother had said he had been mute since birth. The tone changed immediately, since the name to which the child had reacted was that of the place where his grandmother was buried. The mother was shocked to realize it, and then set out to clarify her conflicted relationship with her mother. The sadness she felt after the birth of her child, even though she had wanted him, turned out to be strongly connected to the disappointment she felt at not being able to count on her mother's presence by her side.

It is an understatement to say that this newborn, like so

many others, awakened me to my role as a psychoanalyst: "Listen to me," he let me know in his language, "even though your reason tells you I cannot speak to you. And know that I hear you, even though you think it's beyond me." It is this fundamental message that gave new life to my practice as a psychoanalyst. It is that message I want to convey in this book. At a time when scientific knowledge about the fetus and the newborn is evolving as quickly as the uncertainty about theoretical explanations, it seems important to me to bear witness to what constitutes the effectiveness of psychoanalytic work with newborns. This work has effects that never cease to amaze me.

THE THREE PRISONERS

To explain how it is possible to conduct such a practice, I take as my inspiration principles of action used by psychoanalysts and elaborated by the influential structuralist and psychoanalyst Jacques Lacan through a well-known game of logic: the prisoners' dilemma. A prison warden is considering freeing one prisoner, out of the three who seem worthy to him; his right to grant amnesty is limited to one. Not knowing how to decide who it will be, he leaves it to their sagacity, telling them: "There are three of you here. Here are five disks that differ only by color: three are white and two are black. Without letting you know which I have selected, I will fasten a disk to each one of you, between your shoulders; that is, where you can't see it. . . . Then you'll be given all the time you need to consider your companions and the disk each one is wearing, without being allowed, of course, to communicate the result of your inspection to one another. The first one able to surmise the color of his disk will be allowed to take advantage of the liberation order available to us."[1]

The analysis Lacan gives of this situation goes beyond traditional logic. He posits a three-stage strategy. For the prisoner who wants to come out the winner, he says, what counts in the first place is what is immediately apparent to the senses, what he can observe without reflecting further. In this instance, it is the fact that, if each of the other two prisoners has a black disk on his back, the first prisoner can without hesitation deduce that he has a white disk on his; therefore, he can leave immediately. This immediacy is what Lacan calls *the instant of the gaze.*

The second stage in the strategy is what can be supposed to occur through the mediation of the alter ego. In practice, the prisoner needs a *time for understanding.* The hesitation of the others provides him with information about the color of his disk: If it is black, each of the other two ought quickly to conclude that his is white, and leave; otherwise, both will hesitate. This is the time for an "objective" analysis of the situation.

In Lacan's opinion, the final decision, the *moment to conclude,* presupposes haste; that is, a subjective decision by the prisoner: He must decide the color of his disk without objective proof, lest his hesitation in doing so provide the pretext to one of the other two to do so in his place.

THE APPROACH TO NEWBORNS

Lacan saw these three stages—*the instant of the gaze, the time for understanding,* and *the moment to conclude*—as a model for the psychoanalytic situation. A half-century later, they clarify the approach I had to take toward newborns. For me, *the instant of the gaze* entailed observing what was being done in France for babies born under difficult conditions. Going to see them raised a whole set of problems, practical as well as ethical. I will tell how the experience of Françoise Dolto's psychoanalytic practice with infants in the Antony state nursery and my own experience working with child psychiatrist Caroline Eliacheff initiated my reflections on this subject. I will also speak of the life in the maternity ward headed by René Frydman, of what he set in motion, and of the collaboration with the staff at the Antoine Béclère Hospital in Clamart (a suburb outside Paris). The staff there was a tremendous help in coming up with intervention procedures. I will speak, finally and above all, of what the babies allowed me to see and hear. Unlike the classic psychoanalytic protocol, in fact, where the patient and the therapist do not meet each other's gaze, working with babies begins with the look. And, within the context of the intense emotion that often characterizes childbirth and the days that follow, babies show us almost palpably the problems troubling them.

Being a psychoanalyst for babies has its rules: I had to reconstruct the first principles, without which no proper psychoanalytic work in the maternity ward would have been possible. A psychoanalyst bases herself on a subject's request, which she differentiates from need and from desire. If a patient asks for nothing, if he is there out of a sense of obligation or for the sake of convenience, the psychoanalyst cannot and must not act. How should one proceed, therefore, in a maternity ward, where, by definition, one must go to the patient's bedside? A protocol is required to guarantee the baby and her parents that it will truly be their request that is heard, that they will see the psychoanalyst only if they choose, that they will not be the object of a systematic visit for "psychiatric" evaluation. That is the minimal *time for understanding* necessary for the work to begin. It is obviously possible only because of the many scientific advances made in recent years regarding knowledge about fetuses and infants. It only becomes the more exciting because of them. Researchers in the neurosciences, ethicists, psychoanalysts, but also pediatricians, ultrasound technicians, neonatologists—there is a long list of people who have recently made fundamental and/or experimental discoveries. Without giving an exhaustive account, which would go beyond the scope of this book, I will consider those who have helped establish the foundations of this protocol for psychoanalytic work.

The primary ethical point, the pivotal point of a psychoanalyst's action, remains the following: Every human being is a being of desire, whatever his or her age. Without that postulate, one cannot be a psychoanalyst. How are we to take into account that desire and the unconscious framework within which it is played out? Why, without claiming that the newborn possesses "speech," are we led through psychoanalytic practice to assert that the child thinks? And that her thought is directly connected to the spoken words in her environment, when the latter, provided they are addressed directly to the child, allow her to give meaning to what she is experiencing? Where is the analytical interpretation, and the eventuality of its urgency, located? The replies to these questions, which my position as a psychoanalyst allows me to give, are my *moment to conclude*, and have led me to a certain number of clinical hypotheses. I consider in particular the period of limbo (the four days after birth) and the baby blues (the normal depression that affects new mothers around the third day after childbirth), but also the preventive measures to take, for example, in cases where a child is to be placed for adoption.

A few people—some of them psychoanalysts—have complained about the length of certain psychoanalytic treatments. It is indisputable that, from that perspective, psychoanalytic work with newborns is gratifying, since it very often leads to almost immediate effects. That speed is exciting, since it reassures a psychoanalyst about why she became one. Psychoanalytic treatment is a place of continuous discovery for those who undertake it, including, on occasion, psychoanalysts. That effectiveness is also intriguing and remains to be pondered. Understanding some of the reasons for it already allows us to hear, in the treatment of adults, traces of the "archaic" that had remained mute until that time. As that comprehension becomes sharper, the effectiveness of the psychoanalysis of older children and adults will no doubt increase. In any case, meetings with newborns almost always occur in a context where the human potential for emotions is displayed at its highest level. That is why it is urgent to bear witness to it. I am sure I do not need to elaborate on the emotions I myself felt when I understood that newborns can "converse" with us. I am wagering that readers will recognize the truth of this as well.

1. *The Interests of the Baby*

"Grownups don't understand anything on their own, and it's tiring for children to be explaining things to them over and over again."—ANTOINE DE SAINT-EXUPÉRY

How is the baby doing?

It is common to ask such a question of a friend, but asking it of a society is much more difficult. Are children born under better conditions at the start of the twenty-first century than they were at the start of the twentieth, or does the medicalization of pregnancy and birth reduce the baby and her mother to beings without souls? Does the baby have a cushier spot in the family nest than a hundred years ago, or is she the victim of the shattering of the nuclear family? Has something been gained in proclaiming that "the baby is a person," or are we to believe the historian Philippe Ariès, who claims that the golden age of the child is past? Has the baby gained from the change in gender roles within society, from the working woman and "the new dad"? Or is the baby now only the gnome depicted in Claire Bretécher's comic strips, which depict a baby hung by his suspenders from the coat rack of a baby-sitter in the morning, in a daycare center in the afternoon, and in a fashionable all-night care center in the evening?

On all these points, the responses are not as clear as they seem. It is all a matter of one's personal perspective. To be sure, the infant mortality rate has dropped as a result of advances in medicine. The incidence of childbed fever was greatly reduced in the twentieth century with the establishment of wards in hospitals dedicated to new mothers and their children, and with the introduction of antibiotics; asepsis finally eliminated it. We have come a long way since then. For the baby, the advances are so decisive that, in retrospect, they seem obvious. We are past the time when young children were not given anesthesia "because they don't feel pain." Doctors now know how to distinguish the signs of pain in newborns, and usually succeed in relieving it. What is more, they are beginning to identify the fetus's pain. Birth has not become a risk-free act, however, either from the point of view of affect, or even from a strictly medical perspective. The progress achieved in obstetrics is impressive, and yet we are still at the mercy of disease and accidents. In that respect, Sudden Infant Death Syndrome remains the paradigm for the many unexplained deaths of very young children. It has caught the attention of the general public, and it rightly preoccupies professionals. To prevent it, pediatricians at Béclère, in light of international epidemiological studies, have adopted the habit of recommending that babies always be placed on their backs. In sensitivity training and information meetings on infant care that we hold for mothers who have just given birth, the midwives and I emphasize that method of putting a child to sleep. We can only be very pleased, since we have seen an unquestionable and significant drop in the mortality rate since that recommendation was put into practice. Things are progressing in my own profession as well. Psychiatrists, psychologists, and psychoanalysts are called to the bedsides of new mothers in maternity hospitals to lend them assistance. All these measures make it possible for society to better take into account every new member born into it.

The public knows this and is sensitive to the connections established between the cold world of specialized medicine and the intimacy of the family. The baby no longer has his place only in specialized books arranged on the dusty shelves of the library under *C* for *child care*; he is also the object of many magazines with a wide distribution, each more attractive than the next. The baby is an object of interest. Not a day goes by that you don't hear a mother say: "I was told you have to breastfeed because bottle feeding dehumanizes him," "I read that the baby is sensitive to music and I play *A Little Night Music* for her every evening before going to sleep." And so on. Very often, these rather hasty and personal interpretations have to be tempered, but they certainly demonstrate a new interest in the first years of life.

If legal representation is an accurate reflection of a society, there too the child is gaining respect. In the last ten years, laws concerning the child have been passed: on adoption, confidential childbirth, and the new reproductive technologies. Ethics committees assigned to reflect on the rights of the child and the newborn in society are a sign that the baby's star is on the rise.

As is only right, we applaud these efforts to ensure that the baby "is faring better." Fortunately, France is not a country where babies are bought and sold, and the time is now past when they died of neglect because no one understood their suffering. Let us tone down that tribute, however, since babies, for good reason, do not tell us how they are faring. I am a physician by training, and I know that patients do not always have a say in the diagnosis and treatment of their ailments. That is undoubtedly the reason I became a psychoanalyst. But I still yearn for the great clinicians who sniff out problems by listening to their patients and who know that, in some sense, there is no source more authoritative than the patients themselves. Since the early 1990s, most of my patients have been babies on the maternity ward of Antoine Béclère Hospital, but it took me several years prior to that practice to understand why.

A Professional Journey

A digression by way of my own professional journey will better show how newborns may be of concern to psychoanalysis. Beginning in the mid-1970s, after going to medical school and interning in psychiatry, I had a practice as a psychiatrist for adults in different institutions around Paris; since the 1980s, I have had an office practice as a psychoanalyst. Nothing in my professional life predestined me to take an interest in newborns. I knew nothing about them, or very little. Yes, I had done part of my medical residency on a children's psychiatric ward and was therefore a child psychiatrist, but that was more a supplementary qualification than a sign of any personal interest. Twenty years after the fact, I do not repudiate that necessary ignorance, since there is nothing more terrible than to take oneself for a specialist in childhood. I am still not a specialist in that sense, and I keep my private psychoanalytic practice open to adults. What purpose does it serve to "know" how to listen to a child if one refuses to hear the adult's words celebrating the paradise of childhood? Conversely, how could I claim to assist a newborn without conceptualizing the symbolic place of a social being, a place he will eventually occupy in the world of adults?

What little I knew about children was through their mothers, especially via the cases of baby blues and postpartum depression I had encountered in my practice. Eventually, I founded a study group on the baby blues. A few psychoanalysts were quickly admitted, as were gynecologists and pediatricians. We did bibliographical research on the baby blues and compared our experiences. We composed a questionnaire for mothers. The replies to this questionnaire, which had been distributed in the private offices of gynecologists, were fascinating. We made no statistical claims, of course, but the frequency of certain responses struck us. Hence, when mothers were asked, "Would you agree to speak to a professional about the problems you encountered after your delivery if that service were offered?" they overwhelmingly answered yes. This was particularly astonishing given that, at the time—as is still the case in most public institutions—nothing was set in place a priori for the period following childbirth. Problems affecting the child in the first months were always treated in the pediatric ward; those affecting the mother were, if necessary, dealt with in the psychiatric ward. But nothing specific existed in the maternity ward. Nevertheless, the demand seemed to be there.

A DIRECTION INDICATED BY FRANÇOISE DOLTO

Conjointly with this study group, I had had a practice in a medical-psychological center since 1979. Children were brought in who displayed pathologies ranging from minor difficulties in school to the most disabling psychoses. I tended to see children in the "latency period," between five or six years old and early adolescence. To put things into focus, let us say I became a specialist in bed-wetting, since that symptom is common at that age. But very young children greatly intimidated me; I did not know how to help them.

My colleague Caroline Eliacheff suggested I go with her to observe Françoise Dolto's practice. At the time, Dolto was seeing babies in her office on rue Cujas in Paris whom the Antony nursery had sent her, and who were brought in by their caregiver. These babies, whose mothers sometimes gave birth to them anonymously, were between eight days and three years old. Their mothers were always in social and psychological crisis. I knew of Dolto through the school of psychoanalysis to which she belonged, through her books,[1] and through her radio broadcasts. But it had never occurred to me to learn my profession from her, even though she had about a dozen psychoanalysts studying with her during her sessions with babies.

I wrote to tell her that I wanted to observe her practice. I argued that I wanted to learn how to hear the suffering of babies so as to be able to recognize it in my adult patients. I was summoned to her office. I went at the appointed hour, only to hear from her mouth that she must have made a mistake and that she already had too many women consulting with her. I knew that another applicant had been sent away on the grounds that her competence in child psychiatry had nothing to do with psychoanalysis. A bitter disappointment. I had to bide my time until a "place for a woman" became available, which occurred six months later. As a result, the impatience created in me by that first refusal made me a supermotivated student.

As all those who observed that practice know, she was astounding. As one of them said: "Why, she *believes* in psychoanalysis!" If her practice was formative, it was because she herself was a clinician without peer, with an inimitable way of speaking to children, who very often responded tit for tat. But it was also because she taught that psychoanalysis cannot be taught, and that one had to find in one's own unconscious knowledge the value of what the child throws in your face and of what the theory professes. It was, finally, because she never lost an opportunity to emphasize that the so-called preverbal age, in addition to expressing the archaic, as traditional psychoanalysis claims, also expressed something of spoken language. She spoke to babies a great deal; she thought that speech was exchanged more directly with them than with adults. She also spoke to the psychoanalysts present. She discussed the session that had just taken place, asked us what we had heard. In addition, she made use of our responses; she thanked us or criticized us, depending on the situation. In short, here was a type of transmission to which neither our schooling nor the supervision we underwent with experienced psychoanalysts nor the colloquia we attended had accustomed us.

Dolto helped me enter a field where, shortly before, I would not have ventured. I began to see infants in my practice, and to observe that their symptoms could be relieved after a few sessions, as had been true with her. The suddenness of the effect astonished me. Psychoanalysts are accustomed to thinking that a cure is an extra as far as the treatment goes, and that subjects sometimes have no desire for it, or that such a desire drags on interminably. With babies, everything was sharp and clear. Since I am a psychoanalyst, and a psychoanalyst is still a therapist, there was something in it for me. I was delighted to be able to understand something from the infants in my practice, when a year earlier I would not have understood a single word. In addition, Dolto's passion for teaching reinforced my efforts to listen to these infants and toddlers. I therefore continued; I certainly owed her that much!

Indicative of her devotion to the interests of children, I recall the day shortly before her death when I drove her home after a full morning of sessions. Despite the pulmonary fibrosis that was disabling her, despite the death she knew was imminent, she continued seeing newborns from the state nursery; that was the only activity she kept up. That day, as she had been doing every day for a certain period of time, she was wearing her portable oxygen system and the tube that helped her breathe ("her nose glasses," as she told the children to trivialize the strange machine). She got out of the car with great difficulty and, struggling along, dragged me to a grocery store, asking me to help her carry the apparatus. I resisted: "It makes no sense, you need to get some rest."

"No, no, I'm expecting a visit from my grandchildren, I absolutely must buy some cookies."

That was in Dolto's blood: a passion for children and the strength to live.

After her death in 1988, the sessions with children were supposed to continue; that was her wish, and it became the wish of Children's Services, a state agency in charge of children's issues and of orphans, in particular, on which the Antony nursery was dependent. Caroline Eliacheff was one of the people who agreed to continue the undertaking at the medical-psychological center. I assisted her. For my part, I also saw children already placed in foster families, whom Children's Services sent to me for psychoanalytic sessions.

Although Dolto had freed me from my fear of young children, I did not yet know altogether what they had to do with me. The practice was exciting, in that very young, seriously disturbed children could be released from their symptoms in the space of a few sessions. Despite the fact that these symptoms were extremely severe, they could be reduced in severity as soon as words spoken to the children gave meaning to what, until then, had been the scattered fragments of their history. This was particularly noticeable in children who didn't know their birth parents. It reached a point that, one day, I asked Eliacheff: "If children given up for adoption suffer from holes in language and develop symptoms as a result, and if our intervention makes those symptoms lose their force, might it not be more economical for everyone if we were to intervene earlier, that is, before the symptom appeared?"

The answer was so obvious that she had to say yes. Now we just had to gain access to a maternity ward. It was an attractive idea, but the problem was that no hospital ward in France had ever agreed to pay a psychoanalyst to work with newborns. Who would be adventurous enough to attempt such an experiment?

THE BÉCLÈRE MATERNITY WARD

I had the opportunity to meet Dr. René Frydman, and his open-mindedness led me to ask him to accept me on his ward. Dr. Frydman already ran the maternity ward of the Antoine Béclère Hospital, which was part of the same child and youth services system as the medical-psychological center where I was working and the Antony nursery. A good number of children brought to the nursery were born in that maternity ward. A simple matter of proximity? Not quite. To speak to newborns who are suffering requires, by definition, three elements: babies expressing psychic pain; a psychoanalytic conception of the act of listening; and a place on the cutting edge of technology.

Béclère had a solid reputation for being on the cutting edge. It included a unit pioneering in medically assisted reproduction services, and an extremely specialized department for so-called high-risk pregnancies, combined with a neonatal ward. Later, these wards even became the center of a network of structures around Paris, where the most difficult cases were sent. The staff was renowned. Every new kind of technology was available, and one of the first of the so-called kangaroo units in France was created there.

The aim of the kangaroo unit, more humanistic in its intentions than its name in the literature would suggest, is to allow certain premature babies to remain in contact with their mothers. In every other hospital, premature babies requiring special care are sent to the neonatal ward, while their mothers remain on the postdelivery floor. (If the hospital in question is not equipped with a neonatal unit, the child is transferred to another institution.) The mothers are allowed to visit their babies more or less freely, in keeping with the regulations of each hospital and depending on the type of care required for the children. But they cannot have constant contact with them, and it is very often a major undertaking for them to go to the neonatal unit, especially if they are still recovering from a difficult delivery.

At Béclère, mother and child are hospitalized on the same floor. The idea of the kangaroo unit consists, if you like, of bringing the nursing staff to the babies and keeping the mothers nearby.

The unit serves low-birth-weight babies born full-term, or slightly prematurely; that is, those weighing about four and a half pounds whose care does not require the use of sophisticated technologies. The newborn spends the night in the unit but remains in the mother's room during the day. The mother is sometimes advised to place her child in direct contact with her skin, and an incubator is placed in her room should the baby need it. The staff is responsible for attending to the baby's special needs, but the mother can see her, speak to her, and participate in caring for her at all times. She is even encouraged to do so by the nurses, whose mission is to help the mother take care of her baby when she might feel incapable of doing so because of the child's fragile state.

Because of the success of kangaroo units throughout the world, many published works have studied their impact on the development of premature infants.[2] It is clear that newborns who have been in a kangaroo unit recover quickly, and that the mothers leave reassured and certainly more "competent." In preserving the early relationship between mother and child, the kangaroo unit allows the child to rediscover, after her birth, the prenatal perceptions familiar to her, and hence to develop in greater security. As Françoise Dolto said, a newborn in such a unit has the opportunity to thrive in the *sameness of being*, with no arbitrary break between the periods before and after birth.

For me, these were all signs that the psychoanalytic venture could be attempted in that hospital. When Dr. Frydman's personality is factored in, it is easy to understand how these signs came to constitute a hope. This was not his first adventure. He had been to war; real war in Nicaragua and Palestine, when he accompanied Doctors without Borders and the International Red Cross, but also the war for abortion rights, to which he had offered his contribution as a physician, and even more, the war for in vitro fertilization, since he was one of the scientific "fathers" of Amandine, the first French test tube baby. He was more than a pioneer in all the new reproductive technologies wrongly called at that time "artificial"; he was known as one of the people who had most advanced the ethical reflections on the question of medically assisted reproduction. I might therefore be able to convince this man, for whom birth seemed to be a call for innovation, to attempt an unprecedented experiment.

Things began slowly. First, I was invited to speak at a staff meeting about an undertaking being considered for the maternity ward. Then a letter extended an offer to me to join a study group for psychiatrists and psychologists at the hospital. Finally, I was called in to talk to Dr. Frydman about the advisability of assisting newborns through speech; this resulted in an offer to attempt the experiment for a period of three months. Dr. Frydman soon decided to make that experiment open-ended, so as to officially establish my practice on the ward. He believed it was worthwhile. Although he had not had time to convince himself of the validity of my assertions, at least what the staff was communicating to him seemed favorable. The battle was not over, however, since funds had to be found, and the French agency for mother and child services had refused to subsidize the activity. The policy of the administrative agencies at the time was undoubtedly less bold than the hospital's. I was told in substance that newborns did not need anything, and moreover, that they had not asked for anything. At first, then, I came to work at Béclère as a physician separate from the child psychiatric system. Parallel to my clinical practice, I held meetings there with members of the staff to sensitize them to the specificity of my approach. Then the health services system found it advisable to withdraw its support of me, and the maternity ward stepped in.

A Place for the Psychoanalyst

What does one see on a daily basis in maternity wards, at Béclère and elsewhere? Women in conversation with their newborns. There is, of course, the gurgling of infants responding to maternal caresses, but, more than that, we might also mention the baby blues. They affect almost all mothers to a greater or lesser extent. Over the course of my work at the maternity ward, I have discovered that not only does the baby's presence trigger the baby blues, but that the baby blues summon the baby into language. In other words, contrary to the established practice, a psychoanalyst cannot listen to the mother without listening to the baby, nor speak to one without speaking to the other. I will discuss this at greater length in chapter 5, devoted to the baby blues. But let us already posit that mother and child go hand in hand. I had come to understand, thanks to my study group on the baby blues, that there was a request to talk coming from women; moreover, I had seen the beneficial effects of listening psychoanalytically to very young children. The solution was now to bring the two sides together. Access to both, with no separation between them, had to be achieved. To be sure, mother and child must eventually separate so as not to remain pathologically connected. Each must live her own life. But, precisely for those who have trouble establishing a boundary between themselves and a child they see as a lump of flesh, one must wait until they can negotiate the interdependence of the first days.

NEWBORNS, A SPECIALIZATION?

It is a peccadillo of the mental health professions to divide up the history of individuals into slices. We have child and adolescent psychiatry, which differentiates the psychopathology of one from that of the other (and which would add an infant branch and a newborn subcategory if it were allowed), as well as adult psychiatry and geriatric psychiatry. Some psychoanalysts still insist on marking their specificity as analysts of children or of adults. Of course, the tastes of every therapist and every group of "patients" must be accommodated, but not at the cost of forgetting the continuum of a human being's life. For very young children, separating what the child says from what the mother says, and, in fact, from what the father says, is out of the question. A trace of the status quo, formal and benign no doubt, but real, endures at Béclère: the postdelivery ward is administratively dependent on René

Frydman's obstetrics ward, whereas the kangaroo unit and all the pediatricians in maternity are part of the neonatology ward. Thus, administratively speaking, a mother and her child theoretically fall within the purview of two different units. This is not serious, since usually they will be hospitalized together on the same floor; but the separation remains inscribed. Psychoanalysts moved into hospitals in France many years ago. Until now, however, they only worked during the period before and after birth: before, to aid women with difficult pregnancies or in medically assisted reproduction; after, for problems that emerged in neonatology or pediatrics. There was nothing following "normal" deliveries. Psychoanalysts' priority was to take care of the mothers, not the babies. Very often, that priority included as an implied condition the idea that the baby's symptom was outside their field of competence, that it was medical and pediatric. You don't mix apples and oranges, suffering mothers and babies who supposedly have nothing to say, and, even less, serious matters and doctors of the soul. But here I was, claiming to talk to babies. As a matter of fact, I was simply proposing to transfer what Dolto taught me about babies a few weeks old to newborns a few days old. It was a psychoanalytic matter; that is, an insistence on making speech—in the sense of "making a bull's eye"—out of any articulated symptom that represented a share of unconscious truth. In that respect, psychoanalysis does not inquire about a subject's age or rationality. But it requires a particular protocol, which differentiates it from psychiatry and psychology. This is not exactly the same protocol as that in a psychoanalyst's office, since, in this case, I go to the patient's bedside, but it is certainly a framework that satisfies psychoanalytic criteria.

To understand it, let us consider the list of ailments I deal with in a maternity ward. Newborns suffer from the most varied digestive troubles: they vomit, spit up, have diarrhea or constipation, suffer from colic—some to such an alarming degree that they are placed in danger. They have anorexia, obstinately refuse the breast. They have bulimia, or more exactly, they demand constantly. They cry continuously, day and night. They sleep too much or wake up too frequently. They have skin problems. They have respiratory troubles, minor or grave. They are hypotonic (they have deficient muscle tone or tension); their weight loss after birth does not correct itself after three days, as in normal cases; they are abnormally "lackluster"; they scream, they are overagitated.

Mothers react as they can, depending on their condition and constitution. The professionals reassure them, without fail. What does the psychoanalyst do?

THE GAZE AND THE VOICE

The psychoanalyst must open her ears and attempt to hear the baby, his mother, and his father. When I say this, I have not explained a thing if I don't specify that she is aided in that respect by her eyes. When I enter a room where a mother has called me in, for herself or for her baby, I begin by arranging things so that I can see both protagonists, all three if the father is present, and so that I can be seen by them. The arrangement is different from what we are accustomed to having with adults during an office visit, where the analysand on the couch does not see the analyst, and vice versa. In this case, the first speech organ will be the eye. This means setting in place, through the gaze, a scene in which the newborn is connected to the space of speech as it is taking shape. It means being a witness, looking at the mother, looking at the child, being looked at. In French, the word *regarder* (meaning "look"), which adds a prefix indicating repetition to *garder* (meaning "keep" or "look after"), is derived from the Germanic *wardôn,* which means "wait," "care for." That is truly what is at issue here.

The newborn, it is said, can't see a thing, handicapped as he is by an immaturity of the retinal nerve fibers. But consider the experiments done on the infant's gaze.[3] They have demonstrated that, in a certain way, the child reads lips, that he understands what he sees better than one would think. We also find that he knows how to imitate an adult by sticking out his tongue and opening his mouth, that he mimics the expression of a smiling or grim face. Is this merely a reflexive behavior? Or could the child understand that, when his mother frowns, she is displaying her worry, whereas her smile is a better omen for him? Everything points to the fact that this behavior implies, on the child's part, a symbolic representation beyond the gaze. Otherwise, why would researchers emphasize that a child sees a new object as something *already seen?* Could it be that there is a life before birth, that the newborn has a history? Everyone may raise that question for herself; for the moment, let us be content to take the newborn's gaze as a given.

The psychoanalyst must attempt to let voices be heard. Her own voice, the baby's, the mother's. I have personal reasons for believing so, since my singing background has allowed me to grasp that the voice is truly something of the body coming to life—a glottis, vocal cords, voice box, muscles, breathing apparatus—but also a body beyond itself, moving toward the other who is listening.

Let us go a step farther. As the psychoanalyst Denis Vasse

demonstrates, when the umbilicus closes, the mouth opens: It is a single moment of coming to life. When the cord is cut and the umbilicus called upon to close, the time has come for the child to live in her own body. It is often also the instant of the first wail.

Should the voice of the other rise up, a different dimension opens: "From now on, the baby's relation to the mother as one body to another is mediated by the voice, the baby's voice as well as the mother's or father's. It is in the voice that the rhythmic contact of caregiving comes to be signified, along with the most unconscious inflections this contact produces in parents' hearts."[4] In other words, it is through the voice that the baby is symbolized in the Other, as soon as she is represented, spoken, *vocalized* for the benefit of the other. Through the voice of other human beings, the newborn is no longer simply a body, but a being that has come to the symbolic. The voice is the signifying caesura, more deft at bringing her to life than the cutting of the umbilical cord. It is what names, what distinguishes, and what celebrates the child's body.

That capacity of the voice, inasmuch as it is *heard* by the child in her first moments, henceforth links her for life to two orders that are joined: her body and the history it conveys. The voice in conversation with the infant must therefore be imagined as a force of life.

Regarding the gaze and the voice, let us consider one of Dolto's clinical cases that raises a problem stemming from the period immediately after birth. It involves a child, Frédéric, given up at birth, who refused to learn to read and write. Yet in the drawings he did for the analyst, he painted a multitude of shapes resembling the letter *A*. Dolto was astonished and wondered: Could this be the first initial of the name of someone in his family or of a caregiver? The search seemed to be leading nowhere, when Frédéric's mother revealed that the child's given name before the adoption was Armand. Dolto then explained to Frédéric that it was the pain of early separation that was being scrawled in the *A*'s of his drawings. Once again, she obtained no effect. It was then that she had the intuition to call out to the child for everyone to hear, in an impersonal voice,

> without looking at him, that is, without addressing the person present in his body in front of me, but in a loud voice of a different tone and intensity, turning my head in every direction, looking up to the ceiling, under the table, as if I were calling someone without knowing the space in which he was located: "Armand! Armand! Armand!"[5]

It must have been somewhat like one of the voices of the unknown caregivers he heard in the halls of the nursery before he was adopted. The child suddenly directed his ear toward every corner of the room, not looking at Dolto any more than she was looking at him, until their eyes finally met and she declared:

> "Armand, that was your name when you were adopted." At this, I perceived an extraordinary intensity to his gaze. The subject Armand, once designated, was able to reconnect his body image to that of Frédéric.... It was that reunion through his transference onto me, his psychoan-

alyst, with an archaic identity that had been lost since the age of eleven months, that allowed him, in the following two weeks, to overcome his difficulties reading and writing.

The gaze and the voice: In the first contacts with the newborn, something avails itself to be unraveled.

A Few Days to Listen

The first task in the maternity ward is to realize what is going on. This is not yet the work of a psychoanalyst, but it is preliminary to it, an attempt to grasp the constants within the diversity of details. But what is going on? Inasmuch as "things are not going well" and a woman calls the analyst in to listen to her, the analyst will observe that she is crying, that she is thinking things over, that she is calling, that she is asking, that she is raging, in short, that she is speaking. No fear of the "shrink" can withstand that deluge; this is confirmation of the replies by new mothers to the questionnaire I mentioned earlier. Whenever the nurses and midwives sit down for a moment with new mothers to talk a bit, their efforts are for naught; the mothers are so talkative that the listeners sometimes can't get out of the room. Fortunately, they are compensated, because humanizing their relationship with the mothers makes communication easier and the work more effective. All the same, they appreciate the fact that an analyst can take their place when the need is felt. That opening of the floodgates is nevertheless more a matter of quality than of quantity. The stories evoked by these women, the intimacy and the load of sorrow they contain, prove that something unconscious rises to the surface at the moment of birth and reveals itself or forcefully insists.

That raises a practical problem: There is precious little time to listen to them. A maternity ward such as Béclère, though flexible, keeps a new mother four days at most, seven in the case of a cesarean section. Yet it is on the third day that the mother and child truly begin an exchange. It is often on the third day that the baby blues begin. It is usually at that moment that conflicts appear, as a result of a visit from relatives or because the mother's milk is not coming in properly. Under these conditions, it is sometimes impossible to work effectively, even when hospital stays can be extended "for medical reasons," and even when a mother and baby can come to see me in my office once they have left the hospital. Women used to stay in the maternity ward for two weeks "to rest"; now they have less than four days to get back on their feet. Is this the most intelligent reform that medical progress could have ushered in?

On a more general level, I would like to sensitize those in charge to the idea of a postpartum follow-up in maternity wards. There is a great demand from women in that area. I submit as proof the success of a postpartum practice we opened at Béclère. That practice, reimbursed by the government, is directed at at-risk parents and babies in the months following the birth. Its aim is precisely to compensate for the effect of leaving the hospital too soon and to treat the difficulties experienced by families after the birth that could not be treated earlier for lack of time. The important thing is that it operates in the maternity ward so that patients do not have to formulate a request in a specialized pediatric or child psychiatric ward. We absolutely must recognize that childbirth is a beginning and not an end, and a follow-up must be guaranteed.

LÉA, THE LITTLE GIRL WITH NO NAME

Beyond the gaze and the voice, on the edges of the intense moment following childbirth, the most important thing is the words to be addressed to a newborn. I came to work at Béclère to answer the question: Does intervening with a newborn have any effect? Or, to consider it in terms of a strategy: How can we create the conditions whereby it does have an effect? How can we find the opening through which to speak to the baby? Even before saying why and how, we must see whether it is possible.

Let me cite an example. It is atypical in that it did not present itself bluntly as a massive symptom on the part of the mother or the child. This case, nevertheless, caused a palpable uneasiness, not only for both parents, but also for the nursing staff. As for the child, though she did not say a word, we knew she could not consent to what was happening.

At issue was a woman who had just given birth by cesarean section under somewhat distressing circumstances. She had conceived twins without medical assistance, and had received her prenatal care in a different maternity ward. During the pregnancy it was discovered that one of the twin girls had a very serious malformation. According to her prognosis, she was only expected to survive for a short time after birth. In any event, hospitalization was required. The doctors had enjoined the parents to make a decision about whether to interrupt the fetus's life in utero or to let things remain as they were. The couple was overwhelmed and did not know what to think. They questioned friends who had found themselves faced with a similar dilemma. These friends told them of the hell they had gone through watching their child survive a few weeks in the utmost agony. Horrified, the couple resigned themselves to asking for a selective late-term abortion of the deformed twin, only two weeks before term. As for the delivery, they expressed the wish that it not take place at the same hospital. It therefore occurred at Béclère two weeks later. The mother asked for a cesarean section and obtained it. She was afraid that, if she delivered vaginally, she would find herself face to face with the dead child.

The cesarean section was performed. It should be made clear that, in the case of a late-term abortion of this kind, the dead fetus remains in the uterus until birth. To avoid any toxicity for the second fetus, no epidural is given. The choice is therefore between vaginal delivery without anesthesia and cesarean section under general anesthesia. The mother had no desire to add the suffering of childbirth to her moral suffering. In addition, the dead fetus was supposed to be delivered first, and, as I said, she was afraid to look at it. The request for a cesarean section could thus be justified.

Nevertheless, there was certainly an uneasiness among the nursing staff. They did not judge this mother, since they had learned tolerance through their contact with the tragedies they had so often seen played out at birth. But, though they did not criticize the couple, they needed to confide what they felt rising up in them, and which I would formulate this way: "Who is this lady who demands a cesarean and doesn't want to know anything about her dead child? Who is this couple who decide on an abortion just before term? Couldn't they follow it through to the end?" All the same, I drew the couple's attention to what seemed to me more important as a preventive measure: They needed to indicate to the living twin that her sister was dead and that she would not see her again.

The husband and wife were reluctant to do so and did not feel it was among their duties to speak to the baby. For myself, intervening was out of the question, since, as a psychoanalyst, it is not up to me to anticipate the request, and neither the parents nor the baby were asking anything of me. So, what to do? The baby, from what I know of prenatal shock effects, could be in danger; the parents, without complaining openly, were in denial and confusion; the nursing staff in the kangaroo unit had trouble working calmly with them. If any intervention was possible, it was with the baby, since only she could not conceal the problem from herself. She had several months of companionship with her twin behind her, and that twin had suddenly become inert; then all contact with her had vanished. Nevertheless, I had to refrain from interfering before being called in by the family.

Another problem, apparently minor, then surfaced. The parents could not manage to decide on a name for the living child, which had to be registered with the public records office. The situation had changed, since the parents were thereby manifesting that they could not escape the impasse in which they had placed themselves. I could thus see this as a distress signal. I told the midwife to let them know of my existence and to offer my cooperation in this naming business. They agreed. My notion was that they could not name their living child because they had been unable to name her dead sister. Hers was a death "to be lived" so to speak, and they had to name both babies.

Ultimately, I did not have to tell them this. Between the time they requested I come to see them and the moment I arrived, barely an hour had passed. That interval was sufficient, and the problem was solved; they had named the dead child Sophie and her living sister Léa. Léa, though she had arrived only slightly before full-term, had the look of a very premature infant. It was to her that I first addressed myself: "Your sister, Sophie, whom you had with you in your mother's womb and whose movements you could feel, is dead. That is why, before birth, you could sense she was no longer moving. That is also why you don't see her anymore and why you'll never see her again. Of course, you can keep her memory alive inside you, but she will never again be near you."

Her mother was astonished to hear me speaking to her daughter in that way. Before the medical interruption of the pregnancy, she had asked the doctors whether the remaining child would realize what had happened, but their evasive response left her perplexed. I assured her that the child had certainly perceived sensations relating to that event, and that this was the very reason that words had to be placed over her perceptions.

When I came back to see them three days later, the situation was tense. Léa had lost a great deal of weight. She had had to be force-fed with her mother's milk, but she was spitting up incessantly and everyone was anxious. In the meantime, I had learned from the pediatrician that she was displaying a syndactyly—two of her toes were joined. This is a visible and upsetting malformation, but one that can be cured by a surgical operation later on.

At the time of our second interview, Léa was not in the room, but was being fed in the kangaroo unit. I proposed to the parents that we go find her, and I then told her: "Léa, I have the impression that you wanted to be born but that you have not yet altogether decided to live, and that you are hesitant to eat. To live, you have to eat. You have a malformation of the foot, but it is not as serious as the malformation from which your sister suffered. You cannot die of it; you'll simply have an operation later on, and then you'll have a normal foot."

Then I gave some advice about caring for the child.

I suggested to the nurses that they have Léa taste her mother's milk from a cup. Having a newborn drink from a cup is a "trick" used with premature babies who have not yet succeeded in breastfeeding. In Léa's case, the intention was that she be able to truly *taste* her mother's milk in her presence. I recommended to the mother that she place her child directly on her belly, in contact with her skin, so that the baby could hear the beating of her heart, could rediscover her warmth and her odor. I had her place the child on her left side and her own hand under the baby's sacrum, in such a way as to give the baby a feeling of security that would allow her to drink confidently.

Léa was profoundly depressed; because of her dead twin, she could not manage to think of herself as alive. She had to be led to rediscover her prenatal reference points—her mother's odor and taste in this case—so that she could establish a reassuring continuity between the period before birth and the period after. This was particularly indispensable in that the cesarean section under general anesthesia had deprived her of her first moments with her mother, and she had not had her help in discovering the unknown. It was recovering these sensations, which the separation from her mother had abruptly led her to lose, that would help her be able to think of herself as alive. By that means, she could make the mourning of her sister a "matter of life," and not identify with her in a fatal impulse.

The next day, Léa decided to "save her skin." She began to nurse on her own and in great quantity, which was remarkable given how premature she had appeared. Two weeks later, she left the maternity ward. It was astonishing, given her birth weight. She had clearly taken things in hand. Her ability to save herself came as a relief to the entire staff, which until then had been quite tense, and it also had an effect on her parents. To be sure, they were still in a kind of denial: "Everything that's happening is unfortunately normal; it's because she's premature!"

But they had regained a new energy to care for Léa. It was my duty to respect their defenses, which protected them from too great a sense of guilt. If I had questioned that refusal to see how serious things were, I would have run the risk of compromising the entirely new equilibrium between these parents and their daughter. After all, it is not an easy thing to be expecting two children and to have only one. Now that Léa had given them a new self-assurance, the future lay before her.

That encounter with Léa was decisive, for the staff and for me. It was now a high-stakes game. I had not worked with the parents as I usually do, had not evoked the story of their own parents as I often do. I had banked solely on the words spoken to the child regarding what was her lot in life, and on her understanding. Indeed, however noisy Léa's silence was, it had to be taken at its word. It was a matter of life and death.

But to lift the veil by force, without being invited to do so, would have been to risk not being understood. Because they did not know what to call that little girl, they called me.

The Newborn Is Not an Object of Study

That is how things were at the start of my practice at Béclère. I had before my eyes the effects of the spoken word on newborns. Others were witnesses with me. Doctors who concern themselves with childhood are always astonished to see a psychoanalyst apply her expertise to the so-called preverbal world. Nevertheless, I must say this clearly: I am indebted to the world of research and practical medicine more than to that of traditional psychiatry for my ability to carry on my practice. That is why I wanted to form an organization, La Cause des Bébés (The interests of the baby), in which there could be a cross-fertilization of the viewpoints of these worlds with those of psychoanalysis. In that organization, pediatricians, midwives, neonatal nurses, psychologists, psychiatrists, and social workers, but also neurobiologists, psychophysiologists, obstetricians, historians, and epistemologists set forth their practices and the fruits of their research. In their work, all share an interest in the baby's sensoriality and sensitivity, before and after birth. All question the reification of the child, seen as a sort of unidentified virtual object, an object of every sort of experimental scenario and every form of voyeurism favored by certain kinds of research. All, in a word, treat the child in his dignity as a subject.

Psychoanalysis has often given the impression that it stands apart from hard science, and that it displays through that distance the extent of its contempt for the human body. Thirty years ago, during the heyday of cybernetics, psychoanalysts were accused of claiming to know how the psyche functioned without consenting to open the black box of the brain that would provide its key, as scientists were endeavoring to do. Today they are reproached for denying the organic, even genetic, origin of one mental illness or another, and of covering their eyes when confronted with the discoveries of biochemistry. That view entails a certain misunderstanding. Psychoanalysis does not turn its back on science. It simply challenges the idea that it is rational to consider the human being an object of study. It cannot understand how the human subject can be reduced to the *abolished subject of science* that Lacan condemned in his commentary on Galileo; that is, a subject free of all desire. This is a question of perspective. Moreover, at least since Einstein, who said he would have chosen to be a plumber "if I had it to do over again," scientists have known that they themselves are not free of all desire. Nevertheless, psychoanalysts are not right to complain, since, at least regarding perinatality, the scientific world provides some of the most important support for their theoretical advances. Whether what is at issue is the sensoriality of the fetus and newborn, the acquisition of language, memory, or the body/mind connection, the hopes of modern scientific thought intersect those of psychoanalysis. What is more, they allow psychoanalysis to question in a new way some of the hypotheses it has held for too long. It is that effort of comprehension, which science requires of us and to which it makes its contribution, that we must now consider.

2. A Child Is Born
at Least Twice

"There is no freedom without law.... A free people obeys, but it does not serve; it has leaders and not masters; it obeys laws, but it obeys only laws and it is by the force of laws that it does not obey human beings." —JEAN-JACQUES ROUSSEAU

In Vienna in 1905, Sigmund Freud published his *Three Essays on the Theory of Sexuality*,[1] in which he brought to light children's sexuality. He cast it in a way that made it unacceptable for many, since he gave the very young child the active role of an already independent, if not autonomous, being.

"The child is polymorphously perverse," he wrote.[2] The line has become famous. On the one hand, the child focuses his sexuality on the different erogenous zones—mouth, anus, penis—whose state of excitation he attempts to maintain at a tolerable level. This is the famous theory of stages.

On the other hand, his sexual "responses" to these excitations are suggestive of behaviors that would be called perverted in an adult. The prepubescent child can be, in succession, a voyeur, an exhibitionist, or even a fetishist; he can be cruel or, conversely, masochistic; and so on. Freud describes the infant's onanism in astonishingly precise terms for someone who reconstructed his theories from the memories and words of the adults he had in analysis. He associates these methods of self-stimulation with a certain number of difficulties in infancy—trouble sucking, spitting up, intestinal troubles, etc.—which he sees as a masturbatory method for the child to calm the excitation of the corresponding erogenous zone—the mouth and digestive tract in this case. In all these instances, the child is seen as a person "acting out" his sexuality, and not only as the passive plaything of bodily ailments or influences from the family environment. When Freud speaks of onanism, moreover, he does not fail to describe it as "the execution of a fantasy, that intermediate realm inserted between life lived according to the pleasure principle and life lived according to the reality principle."[3] For Freud, what takes precedence is the underlying fantasy, the way the child elaborates on his sensations, and the *sexual theories* he constructs. Whatever errors mar them, Freud says, it is these theories that allow the child to give meaning to corporeal excitations or perceptions that are beyond his control. To be precise, he says, it is his way of replying to the question: Where do babies come from?

This applies, of course, to children at least three years old, and is therefore not pertinent to my subject. But, regardless of the age problem, an intangible principle can be drawn from the content of these two theses and the controversies to which they have given rise, a principle Freud put forward from the beginning, namely, that the child reflects, elaborates, acts out his life, and, in the first place, his sexuality. In that respect, he is active and desiring, and to fail to recognize this about him would be worse than taking the wrong path:

It would be going nowhere. In that sense, all psychoanalysts are midgets standing on the shoulders of a giant. The tremendous advances of those who came after Freud and who concerned themselves with the earliest ages—Anna Freud, Melanie Klein, Donald Winnicott, and Françoise Dolto, to mention the best known—would not have been possible if they had not gotten that first imperative from Sigmund Freud. The step we now need to take is to recognize that the newborn was born before being born, or, more precisely, that her life had already begun nearly nine months earlier, that she knows this in her own way, and that this is meaningful for her from the first day.

The Newborn's Sensoriality

HOW TO GIVE MEANING TO ONE'S LIFE

The newborn gives meaning to his life with the means at his disposal, and a psychoanalyst's first imperative is to recognize this. Here is one example, among a thousand that reached my ears in the maternity ward.

Raphaël, barely three days old, suffered from painful diarrhea. That situation is common among infants, whose digestive system is not mature in the first moments of life. But this particular diarrhea resisted treatment. It put him in a state of pain, tears, and screams, intolerable even for members of the staff who were inured to such things; and his weight was dropping at a dangerous rate.

"There's nothing to say, everything's going well except for that diarrhea!" commented his mother, who had nevertheless asked to see me. For a time, she had suffered from anorexia, and the advent of the pregnancy led to some contortions on her part. Draconian diets, nausea, fantasies of inducing an abortion; she used every means at her disposal to maintain, in her own eyes, a certain ideal of a flat belly. Sometimes, she even cursed this child who was making her "enormous," despite the desire and anxiety she felt for the baby she was expecting. My discussion with her led her to talk about the problems she had identifying herself as a wife and potential mother, but the important thing was, in the first place, to take the child as a witness.

I thus told Raphaël in substance that, though his mother had had these thoughts of evacuating him in some sense, she had abandoned that wish; that she even seemed particularly happy to have been able to overcome it in order to welcome him. Therefore, to be fully accepted by her, he, Raphaël, did not need to conform to that wish by "evacuating himself" by his own means, as if he were only a waste product of his mother and not a baby. That message in itself was not enough to explain how his symptom came to disappear the same day, since the conversation included other elements. But it constituted the initial point of contact that allowed him to move on. Without that preliminary recognition of the meaning he was giving to his precarious presence and existence, the dialogue might not have been established.

The foundation of a practice with newborns is this: The baby attempts to give a meaning to what he is experiencing, whatever the conditions of his birth, even when everything is new for him out in the open air, where he still has trouble thriving.

How to give that meaning a chance to be heard, when no

one manages to recognize it? How to proceed in such a way that this meaning can be saved should it come to be missing? How to give safe haven to these attempts at communication by the newborn, when the immediate environment cannot provide it for various reasons?

The response is not simple; in fact, it is still a work in progress, because of the extremely rapid evolution, in the last twenty years or so, of scientific knowledge about the fetus and infant. Research has resulted in new, fundamental discoveries, which in turn have fostered the development of new techniques, which then have contributed toward the emergence of new theoretical hypotheses. For the fetus, things are particularly clear: where there were only conjectures in the 1970s, the evolution of embryology and genetics has allowed new prenatal approaches to be developed. Ultrasound technology has brought astounding changes to diagnostic procedures and prenatal care; research in the psychophysiology of the fetus and the newborn has led to new preventive measures; and the technologies of medically assisted conception have revolutionized the situation of many infertile couples.

At the Antoine Béclère maternity ward, we are the witnesses to, as much as the privileged agents of, these advances. Paradoxically, this progress complicates matters after childbirth. The more one knows at a medical level about fetuses, newborns, and new mothers, the more medicalized hospital care becomes, and the greater the risk that no room will be left for the words of the individuals involved. In this, I am not slipping into the facile overreaction of claiming that the hospital environment infantilizes women patients. That is wrong. On the contrary, consideration of this matter has advanced a great deal in France, and I can attest to the fact that, at Béclère, many doctors, midwives, and nurses perform their duties with utmost respect for the dignity of new mothers and babies. The problem is more difficult to approach because it is institutional.

PREMATURE BABIES

Let us take the example of premature births. Premature babies born at twenty-six weeks are often viable from a medical point of view, but clearly require continuous care that cannot be provided on the ward where women recover from "normal" deliveries. These babies are therefore separated from their mothers and placed in intensive care in the neonatal unit, located in a different wing of the hospital. The babies' weight may be very low (sometimes less than a pound); their pulmonary and neurological systems are still underdeveloped; they need assistance at all times in a unit where everything is done to facilitate their development outside the mother's womb. What about the mothers? The mothers wait alone in their rooms in the maternity ward. Sometimes they do not even know exactly whom they are waiting for, because they gave birth under general anesthesia and the child was transferred to the neonatal unit before they were able to see her. They therefore gaze again and again at the fuzzy Polaroid of the child who was handed to them. Dubious or anxious, they try to connect that image of a virtual being invaded by strange tubes to the flesh-and-blood baby they were expecting. Of course, they will be able to visit the child, but they will have to wait until their own condition is judged acceptable. For the moment, they expect the worst or the best, de-pending on their state of mind. It is striking, when I talk to mothers of very premature babies, to see the force of their *primary maternal preoccupation*—in the expression of the psychoanalyst Donald Winnicott[4]—to see how intense their concern for their child is, even though it occurs in a vacuum. They imagine, often judiciously, the particular care their child's situation will require from them. But, unable effec-tively to provide it during the separation, they resign them-selves and become depressed.

"I'm a bad mother, incapable of helping him just when he needs me most. You're a psychoanalyst, you know the first moments are decisive," said one mother, choking up in her powerlessness.

"I wasn't even able to carry him to term . . . it's all my fault," another said, outraged.

"What good will it do to go see him and talk to him? They told me he has tubes in his mouth and nose—so how could he recognize me?" complained another.

"I'd only be a bother," said another woman, who had reached the point of apologizing for her maternal love. "In any case, they told me I'm very weak myself. The nurses in intensive care will do things better than I could."

When I began my practice, I replied to these women and to the others dispossessed of their primary maternal preoc-cupation by the power of medical technology in terms of what I knew about the situation of premature babies. I prac-ticed "educative medicine," to use Dolto's term. I explained that these premature infants, even more than others, needed the presence of their mothers and fathers, that, even more than others, they would be sensitive to that presence and would recognize it. I told them it had been proven that the newborn recognizes her mother's presence and voice from among a hundred others,[5] that she has a memory of the timbre and low frequency of the father's voice, that, to a great extent, she discerns the mother's bodily odor and the taste of her milk. I explained to them how the words they gave their baby established a connection with her, how important it was that they be able to name her, speak to her of her brothers and sisters, tell her the particular context of her birth and pregnancy; in short, all the signifiers necessary for the child to construct herself.

Of course, the mothers would have said all that to their child under normal conditions. The child would have been soothed by the mother's words in their day-to-day dialogues or during family visits. Here, unfortunately, that was not possible. However much the parents may have wanted it, the separation imposed by medical necessity risked creating a vacuum of words, a hole of language around the child. I therefore suggested that they visit the child as often as possible to fill the gap, except when that was contraindicated for medical reasons; that they speak to him, sing lullabies if they liked, caress him, in place of the care they could not give him. I taught them to notice when the baby opened his eyes and sought communication, and when, on the contrary, he showed he was tired and that they could stay beside him but not disturb him. In short, I tried to give them the maximum number of elements that would allow them to evaluate and respect their child's capacity for concentration, which, though intense, is weak.

At the time, I was rarely witness to the effect my advice

may have had on the babies, since it was unusual for me to have access to them. At best, I heard what the mothers reported when I happened to see them again. By contrast, what I saw at every turn were the mothers' radiant faces at the end of our conversation, their relief in finding a living justification for their maternal solicitude. In the end, I told myself that this type of intervention was not solely pedagogical, and that I should not limit myself to responding to particular requests.

If the problem for these parents was how to be a mother (or a father) to a premature baby, how to practice parenting, then we had to work toward systematic prevention, without departing from the principles of psychoanalysis. The goal was not only to improve the self-esteem of women who no longer felt they played much of a role in their child's arrival, but to encourage them to exert their primary maternal preoccupation. Above all, the aim was to not deprive the child himself of the primordial elements that ensure his growth, even apart from any medical considerations. Now, with the consent of the staff, I systematically visit the rooms of mothers whose children are in intensive care. The information I give is preventive, so to speak; it is particularly needed at Béclère Hospital, where cases of separation of this type are not unusual.

A SENTIENT INFANT

But whether babies are premature or not, it is reassuring to know that all babies are born with a complete sensorial foundation. Scientific research is showing us this.[6] Everything is in place at birth.

The Recognition of the Voice

A newborn recognizes his mother's voice as being the same as the one he heard filtered through the abdominal wall, hence distorted, during pregnancy. He also recognizes the voice of his father or of the man who was with the mother, provided he spoke near the mother's belly, or directly and distinctly addressed the fetus during the pregnancy. Since T. Berry Brazelton, a pioneer in the field of research on the newborn's hypersensitivity, almost everyone has been in agreement about this. Further verification of this has been found by Marie-Claire Busnel, a researcher in acoustic physiology who has found that the newborn's heart rate slows while the mother is speaking and—an even more convincing result— when the mother speaks *to it*. Other researchers have relied on the increase in sucking reflexes, not provoked by hunger, under the same circumstances, still others on the frequency of motor responses to the mother's words (a fetus turns its head toward the place from which the voice is emitted, opens its eyes, move its arms).

All reach the same conclusion: A child only a few days old reacts to language stimuli more than to other types of stimuli, even though she supposedly does not understand a word of it. While still a fetus, she learned to distinguish the voice of her mother from background uterine noise, other sources of external noise, and even the voices of other people. As a newborn, she recognizes that voice from among those of other women, prefers it, and recognizes it as coming from the same woman she heard in utero. In addition, after birth, she recognizes the language her mother is speaking, whereas she does not react to a language she never heard during the pregnancy. What does this mean? The fetus discriminates between the syllables of the mother tongue. It is as if the newborn had at her disposal a stock of phonemes for the language heard during the pregnancy, and was "preformed" at birth for that language. That preformation remains in force for about six months, during which time the child retains a preference for her mother tongue. The term "mother tongue" is to be taken literally. This obviously would not prevent the child from learning a great number of languages, but she will maintain her preference.

Does that mean she speaks our language? Not at all, and no psychoanalyst or researcher would venture to say so. She speaks, I will say half-jokingly, like a deaf person. Two researchers in another field, psycholinguistics,[7] have demonstrated that children born profoundly deaf, children whose parents are also deaf and therefore use sign language, begin to *babble with their hands* before mastering sign language. They compared the manual activity of two deaf babies and three hearing ones, aged between ten and fourteen months. They took care to differentiate their ordinary gestures (for example, holding out their arms to be picked up) from their "hand babbling," that is, gestures without apparent motivation. Result: Hand babbling represented more than half the activity of deaf children, versus only 10 percent for the hearing children, and it led through the normal stages to the appearance of the first word signs. Newborns, deaf or hearing, are therefore not mute, in the sense that, upon arriving among us, they already have a minimal repertoire and are apt to generate, to construct, a language. In other words, they speak before knowing how to speak, they try out babbling before having an ad hoc semantic and lexical repertoire. We won't say they understand what they are doing, or what we are saying to them; that's a hard task. For the moment, let us be content to observe that they have the means for understanding and for emitting messages, and that these messages may have a meaning. It is our job to discover it.

"The cloth that smells Mama-good."

Although the sensorial foundation is already present at birth, and fetuses and newborns already have a significant sensorial lived experience, nothing is settled for good, since the newborn needs his parents to make the connection between his sensations before birth and after. The slightest break in that connection presents difficulties when he constructs himself.

Mrs. Perrier was referred to me because she had not stopped crying for several days, and she wanted to speak to me about it. She was a first-time mother, and her tears in no way encroached on her joy about having that child. She had no complaints about her daughter. It so happened that this daughter, Marie, had a slight case of jaundice, which required phototherapy. The treatment consisted of exposing the child to bright light, for as many four-hour sessions as it took for the jaundice to disappear. She was placed nude and blindfolded in a sort of hammock, and was left that way under the glare of the lamps. In itself, there was nothing violent about the therapy, except the luminous ambiance, undoubtedly somewhat disconcerting for a little girl who had just spent nine months in relative darkness. The equipment was rather impressive, the nakedness and blindfold relatively unsettling. Hence babies sometimes displayed discomfort with the situation, even though the treatment was painless and fairly routine. Marie found the treatment unbearable. Her screams and cries caused panic in her mother, who, defenseless, saw that the only solution was to cry along with her. All this was so disturbing that the nursing staff recommended to the mother that she meet with me.

That child was separated from the first person she had ever known. Here again, I had only to keep in mind experimental protocols to understand that she was missing something that would allow her to form a link to all the new sensations coming at her from strangers and unprecedented situations. No, Mrs. Perrier was not being thoughtlessly "sensitive" to her child's discomfort by crying constantly. No, Marie was not statistically abnormal for reacting poorly to the jaundice treatment. Yes, she needed to rediscover familiar sensations in order to face situations with which she was unfamiliar. It was for Marie and her mother that I had to invent a separation procedure, in such a way that Marie could use her natural sensitivity as a reference point, rather than let it become a source of anxiety. I therefore proposed to the mother that she inform her daughter when the treatment was coming, explain the reason for it and how it would unfold, and give the name of the nurse to whom she was to be entrusted, allowing her to identify the nurse's voice. I also suggested that she indicate to the child that her mother would see her again in four hours.

I now advise that procedure for all mothers temporarily separated from their newborns. What is the point of knowing that the heart and breath rate of a newborn changes when he hears his mother's voice among several others, what is the point of knowing he searches for that voice by opening his eyes and turning his head, if we do not make use of that knowledge in such simple prophylactic situations as these?

Mrs. Perrier went to see Marie and, as I had suggested, placed a cloth bearing her odor near the girl's face. We have known the importance of the newborn's sense of smell since at least the 1950s. Newborns have a particularly acute sense of smell, although they lose this acuteness later on.[8] In addition, newborns have a significant olfactory memory, and the presence beside them of a cloth permeated with their mother's odor is powerful reassurance when she is gone. Marie was thus able to smell that cloth near her, and even to snuggle up to it. That little girl, who four days earlier had been bumping against the walls of her mother's womb, now found herself in a vacuum under the lamps, with no contact with anything, no point of reference. She had not yet reached the age when a person has a clear perception of the limits of her own body. That simple cloth was surely able to serve as an edge for her, just as the edges of a crib allow the infant to "settle in." In any case, Mrs. Perrier came back to see me an hour later. She was glowing, and told me that the session that day had gone wonderfully well and that Marie had slept peacefully in her hammock.

Why does the sense of smell have such importance for the infant? Probably because of a cortical substratum that is particularly well developed at that moment in her life. The importance of the rhinencephalon, the chiefly olfactory part of the forebrain, which will later regress, temporarily makes the infant a genius at smelling. From the neurophysiologic point of view, this is a minor riddle. Let us ask it this way: Everyone has had dreams containing more or less fantastic images, lively music, more or less agreeable physical contact, or the taste of strange food. But no one wakes up from a dream with the memory of a particular odor, its mellowness or sharpness, its power, its sweetness. It seems that, unlike other sensations, smell is not processed and committed to memory through the thalamus, the structure held to be the principal mechanism for a certain kind of affective memory.

What does a baby do, then? We know that, in burrowing into his mother's breast, he seeks as much to breathe in the maternal odor, that of her body and milk, as to satisfy his hunger. Has he committed to memory these odors, which he "tasted" by swallowing the amniotic fluid during his intrauterine life? The mother's odor, and the flavors of whatever she eats, pass into her blood and into the amniotic fluid. Do newborns behave like "noses," those professionals who develop perfumes and can stock their memories with two or three hundred different fragrances, in a manner still incomprehensible to science? Neurophysiologists will find the answer to that still-unexplored riddle. A psychoanalyst must consider the newborn's sense of smell as one of the first connections to her mother, along with the sucking and swallowing associated with it. It is there, in the bodily intimacy between mother and child, that the child begins to construct herself. Her own body is connected to the breast as a source of pleasure; her idea of her own body, of her mouth that sucks and emits sounds, of her nose that smells, of her lips that suck, of her ears that hear the familiar voice, all hang on that mother's odor. If the mother disappears without explanation, the child's assurance about her own body is called into question. That is why it is indispensable that words come to fill that absence, whatever the reason for it. In Marie's case, it was an easy matter and the effect was rapid, because it was the mother herself who could explain to her daughter the reason for her temporary absence. There are cases when that is not possible, when the child is placed for adoption or when the mother has an accident or dies. Is that not what Dolto had in mind when she evoked a

> wound in the subject's relation to its own body, because the image of the body is amputated from an erogenous zone that departed with the mother, and which was the baby's sense of smell and the act of swallowing? That image of the body can be restored to the subject if one brings it, so to speak, materially or subtly, the odor of the mother remaining on her clothing. What comes back to life at that time is the subject's body, its fundamental image of its own body; it is the image of functionality, the possibility of sucking; whereas, without the mother's odor, the subject no longer knew, for example, how to suck or swallow.[9]

It is clear why the child needs to be reassured of an "olfactory continuity."

Further Thoughts on the Method

Mrs. Perrier was so satisfied with my advice and with the effects of the measures she took with Marie that she seriously wanted me to return before every treatment session. Obviously, I declined the offer, since that would have led her to believe in a "magic" effect of such interventions, whereas she needed to see that she could have the same effectiveness.

That is because, for a patient, there is less to be expected from the person of the psychoanalyst than from the workings of the psychoanalytic framework. The patient can expect that the laws, the procedures set in place, and the rules of operation will liberate her from obedience to human beings (the person of the psychoanalyst in this case) and will allow her to obey only laws, as Rousseau said. That is why a procedure like this one is so important.

This procedure might seem to some people to be a detail or a ritual. That is not the opinion of the members of the nursing staff, who directly reap its benefits and say so. According to the psychoanalyst Lucien Kokh, whose theoretical reflections were a great help to me in elaborating the crucial points of my practice, a procedure of this kind is "the condition sine qua non for making the word present." Without it, it is difficult to reestablish the broken links in the chain of communication between infant and mother. The psychoanalytic framework is there to allow the mother to remember, if anyone wished to make her forget, that speaking is the human means of communication par excellence. Why should she deprive herself of it on the pretext that her child is not mature? Because she would be accused of indulging in a rambling monologue?

In terms of the systematic visits I make to the mothers of premature babies, I am pleased at the invigorating effect the procedure can have. It is rare that the mothers remain depressed after such visits, and when they do, other, deeper causes are at play. Most of the time, they even recover an eagerness that must be restrained: They want to rush over to the neonatal ward to see their baby, but their condition requires precautions (particularly in the case of women who have had cesarean sections). It is this renewed desire for life on the mother's part that will sustain the premature baby's desire through the difficulties he must face.

The treatment for jaundice has evolved somewhat since Mrs. Perrier's experience. Portable sunlamps are now set in place in the mother's room; the mother is present and the problems alleviated. But the procedure remains valid for other treatments requiring separation from the mother.

These procedures are exceptions to the general treatment protocol I will discuss later on. In this case, I intervened systematically; in the others, I intervene only upon request. In both cases, the aim is to hold onto the intrapsychic sensorial relationship that existed before birth between mother and child, and to see that the normal operation of the hospital ward does not prevent the mother's words from complementing, as it were, the newborn's sensoriality.

When the psychoanalyst intervenes with babies in the maternity ward, she is not a scientist; she is a practitioner of the word. She remains faithful to the fact that psychoanalysis is, as they said in Freud's time, a talking cure. Or, to quote Lucien Kokh's words—excerpted from a private tape recording: "Whoever holds a position as practitioner of the word, whoever acts on his conception of a thesis in the practice of the word, *cannot be the same* as the person who undertakes an evaluation. Within the framework of the unconscious, one cannot be both inside [that is, listening to what is not said in everything we are told] and outside [that is, attempting to evaluate whether what is unsaid has reasons for being said or is null and void]." That is logical. We are not studying an object about which we must say something, we are listening to a speaking subject. It is not the same job. In doing so, let us keep in mind what psychoanalysis owes to artistic creativity, recalling a sentence by novelist and art theorist André Malraux that was repeated when his remains were buried at the Panthéon: "It is not passion that destroys the work of art, but the desire to prove."

Repetition

"But you know, I feel fine living like this," Mrs. Cohen told me, bursting into tears.

These were her first words after greeting me. She had agreed to see me because one of her sons was constipated, and no treatment had been effective. She was not doing so well as all that, apparently, and she immediately told me about her life over the previous months. She had given birth to twins a week earlier. When she learned she was going to have twins, she had a violent reaction: "One child is all right, but two!" She was herself a twin and had suffered enormously from being constantly obliged to yield the spotlight to her twin, who was showered with praise by her parents, whereas she was denigrated. History seemed to be repeating itself, and that was too much for her. She therefore asked for an abortion. Then she reconsidered, changed her mind again, returned to her first point of view, hesitated again. Finally—was it the sight of the ultrasound image?—she decided to keep her two children. And, excessively demanding of herself, she decided that, since she had made that choice, she ought to be happy with it. Hence the content of her contradictory declaration: I'm crying but I feel just fine.

It occurred to me that the constipated child in question was only repeating his mother's denial by putting into play his body, his privileged means of expression. He was very calm, despite the unpleasantness that his constipation, resistant to all treatment, must have been causing him. There again, everything was just fine. He too had a decisiveness that nothing could deter: He refused to drink and to have bowel movements. I therefore told him: "Your mother says she feels just fine living like this and, at the same time, she's suffering. You seem to be telling us the same thing: You're calm, you're fine, but you refuse any exchange with your mother. You ask nothing of her when you're hungry, you give her nothing when you're full."

At these words, the mother suddenly realized that she never waited for her child to ask to suckle before feeding him. His brother called for her, she fed him, and she took the opportunity to wake the other twin and breastfeed him, without saying a word and without his asking for anything. That situation is common with twins—it is so tiring for a mother to get up twice as often during the night—but it is not sufficient to trigger a symptom, as it did here.

What was this child doing? He was *effacing himself,* as his mother must have effaced herself in the past. Not only did he put his mother's denial to his own use, but he replayed the desire for an abortion she manifested at the very beginning of her pregnancy. She only wanted one child, hence he was giving up his place. He was surviving, but he did not demand or give anything; he existed, but just barely; he was not gaining weight. Something on that order was being played out for him, it seemed to me, and I told him: "Your mother was afraid at the start of her pregnancy to have two children and not one. For a time, she considered not keeping both of you. But that didn't last, she changed her mind. That's why you were born, you don't need to efface yourself. . . . You want to act like your mother with her sister? But you're not your mother's sister, you're her son." I then verbalized other elements of his family history, whose details I will refrain from giving. The main thing is that they allowed him to draw an outline of his familial space and thus to remove it from the cluster of parental fantasies related to being a twin.

The child had a bowel movement an hour later, with no help from the prune juice that is often used to stimulate newborns' intestinal tracts. The administration of said juice had, in fact, failed in this case.

Such clear results are impressive. Even when you've seen a large number of that kind, they always leave you flabbergasted. Nevertheless, they raise formidable questions. The first has to do with the connection between psychic life before and after birth. We know we are dealing with the same being "before" and "after," but the question is whether he himself bears a trace of that knowledge; that is, whether the prenatal events that concerned him are part of his postnatal baggage. Having said that Mrs. Cohen's child was replaying his mother's desire that he efface himself by complying with it through his symptom, I need to make explicit the scope of such a repetition.

AN INELUCTABLE CONSTRAINT

Repetition—"the invariable lament of the wind one hears day and night, always uttered in the same tone"[10]—is a problem that haunts the history of psychoanalysis and the offices of its healers. It accounts for the peculiar fact that, in analysis, people have a tendency to return to the same impasses, the same behaviors, or the same discourses as those that motivated them to enter analysis and that continue to trouble them.

Mr. X, who could not understand the haughty and distant uneasiness he felt, against his will, toward his son, recounted that he made a point of formally receiving each of his children in his office every Saturday. Without realizing it, he was replaying a memorable scene from his childhood, in which his own father had heaped scorn on him in his office, in front of his brothers and sisters. He was forgetting only one ingredient, which the analysis of the repetition led him to rediscover. This was the word "contempt," which his father had used that day in reference to him, and the "quarantine" that had followed. For a time, he was forbidden to share in the games of his brothers and sisters. Something persisted as a muffled echo of that contempt and the quarantine to which he had submitted; namely, the haughty and distant attitude he displayed toward his own son. In another case, a woman was constantly forgetting her apartment keys, until a question from her analyst made her suddenly remember that she had been born in Trousseau (which means "set of keys") Hospital, and that someone had told her she had been "misplaced" on the ward for a few minutes.

The funniest and the most tragic examples illustrate this phenomenon of repetition. It is as if these people keep bumping up against something. They do not know where that compulsion to repeat is coming from, and instead of remembering what might have motivated it, they play out a scenario that remembers it for them. Freud considered that insistence an automatism, a constraint. Its coercive aspect is particularly marked, given that the return of memory through repetition can be constrained by the logic and automatism of language itself. Hence, the association *lost keys-Trousseau-misplaced* indicates a preconstrained path to the solution of the riddle. Think more generally of situations where, the more you try to get away from an idea, the more the words you use impose it.

So much for the automatism of repetition. Repetition is also the result of an unpleasant encounter, an encounter with a piece of the unbearable *real*, a piece of data unassimilated as such by the subject: the disconcerting encounter with a father in his office, for example. More generally, since Freud linked repetition to the death drive, it is the encounter with a ghost that slips furtively along the horizon of forgotten memories. I opened this section with the words of the philosopher Sören Kierkegaard, who made repetition into a concept by attaching to it the allegorical figure of the wind. Let us allow the novelist Claude Simon to spin out the same metaphor, so that we can see the horizon this metaphor reveals: "Soon [the wind] would blow into a storm on the plain . . . a force unleashed without aim, condemned to exhaust itself endlessly, without hope of end, moaning at night in a long complaint, as if it were lamenting, envying sleeping men, transitory and perishable creatures, for their capacity to forget, to be at peace: for the privilege of dying."[11]

The "Organic Clock"

This thesis of an unassimilated piece of data repeated through the symptom is very useful in the practice of analysis. It makes it possible to grasp an idea suggested to Dolto through her clinical practice and discovered by Freud's friend and collaborator Sándor Ferenczi—an idea, it seems, that has gotten little response in the scientific literature. That idea is chronological repetition. That is, a newborn's symptom at time X of his postnatal life may correspond to a traumatic event that occurred at time Y of his prenatal life, as if the child were recalling an event that took place during the second month of pregnancy, for example, and, like a clock, displayed a symptom that evoked that memory in the second month of his postnatal life. It should be understood that this triggering event concerned him, that he directly perceived it through his mother, or that it was indirectly generated by his father.

An acceptable idea? Reason says no. No experimental verification has come along to confirm it. Practice says yes, however, and the number of coincidences of this type, though they may seem misleading to some, is nevertheless evident. Dolto gives a few examples of "organic clock children" of this extremely precise kind. So long as scientists take no interest in this thesis, not even, potentially, to fine-tune it, it is unreasonable to disregard such a sign when one has knowledge of it. Nine times out of ten, it entails missing an opportunity to deliver the newborn from a repetition that threatens her. In the same way, we might say that the "word holes" marking a newborn can pop up at adolescence. Listening as psychoanalysts to newborns is also a method for preventing a troubled adolescence.

FROM FETUS TO INFANT, A CONTINUITY

Some have asked that we stop using the term *fetus* for what ought to be considered simply human babies before their birth. The psychoanalyst Bernard This believes that, in using

that word, we run the risk of not respecting the human beings they are, a risk reinforced by the alibi of technical
language. It is an important reminder, since it suggests
unequivocally the human subject's continuity of substance
and existence from conception on. We have seen that this
is true at the level of sensoriality. I wish to show that it also
affects the connection the child establishes with his mother.
Nevertheless, I will continue to speak of "the fetus," since,
let us recall, birth is not simply a change of residence or
environment.

Without making reference to the psychoanalytic clinic,
we can discuss pre- and postnatal repetition by observing fetuses and infants. Contrary to a general belief, the baby in
utero and its mother are not a single entity. A wall separates
them, the trophoblast and the placenta. It is only a slight
difference, some will say, the thickness of a sheet of tissue paper. No thicker, in fact, than the boundary separating truth
from error.

The difference, though, allows us to reconsider a few received ideas. There is no *fusion* between mother and child,
either physical during pregnancy or psychic after birth.
Nothing of what has been said in that regard is based in reality. By the end of the pregnancy, moreover, the fetus and the
mother no longer live by the same rhythms.[12] Although at
the beginning of the pregnancy, it is the ovarian hormones
that sustain the fetus, by the third month the placenta is
sufficiently mature to replace them. Since the placenta is part
of the child's corporeal integrity, this is a first glimmer of the
child's autonomy in relation to its mother. The fetus now
secretes on its own the hormones necessary for its growth.
This is true to such an extent that a woman whose ovaries

have been removed can sustain a pregnancy, provided she is given a substitute hormonal treatment during the first three months; beyond that, the now-functional placenta will assume control of operations.

The baby/fetus already has a share of autonomy. A study has been undertaken on this subject by the Italian psychoanalyst Alessandra Piontelli. That work—dense, exciting, and still incomplete—turns entirely on the continuity between intrauterine life and infancy. A child therapist and professor at the famous Tavistock Clinic in London, a visiting professor in the department of child psychiatry at the University of Turin, she also has a private psychoanalytic practice in Milan. In addition to that work, she has begun a program of observation and research on the period prior to and immediately following birth. Wishing to give herself a new, high-yield means for completing the study, she chose to follow a single group of children, using ultrasound technology during pregnancy and observing mother and child in the five years after birth.[13] Her work is filled with notes and revelations that are extraordinarily disconcerting for most of us. I confine myself to drawing attention to two themes she develops, which intersect our inquiry into pre-/postnatal repetition: the poorly explained phenomenon of infantile amnesia, and the study of twins.

In the matter of twins, whom Piontelli has studied at length, she explains that her attraction to them stemmed from a short-term therapy she practiced long before her research and that marked her profoundly. At issue was an intelligent and sensitive eighteen-month-old child. His parents had brought him to her office because he was sleeping very little and could not stand still for a minute all day long. He was driving them crazy.

In her office, Piontelli immediately noticed that he had begun to rummage through every corner of the room, visibly in search of something he could not find. His parents confirmed that he spent his time at home on similar investigations, day and night. They added that, every time he learned to make a new movement—to sit up, crawl, etc.—he seemed to do it with an intense fear, as if, they said, he were afraid of "leaving something behind."

Piontelli noted another repetitive behavior on his part, which consisted of shaking various objects found in the room, the way one shakes someone to wake him up. She decided to speak directly to the child to tell him what she was feeling, namely, that he seemed to be looking for a lost object that he despaired of ever finding again. The child, she said, abruptly stopped his little game and stared at her for a long time. She took advantage of his uncustomary attention to say she had the impression he was shaking objects as if he were afraid they were dead. At these words, his parents burst into tears, explaining that this eighteen-month-old child, Jacob, was the twin of little Tino, who had died in utero two weeks before term. Jacob was thus still looking for Tino, and was leaving no stone unturned. Had he shaken Tino in his mother's womb the way he grabbed the objects in the therapist's office? We do not know. But Piontelli explains that a great change came over Jacob from that moment on, and that she needed only a few sessions to tell him again of the intense guilt about his brother's death that accompanied each of his acts. As for the parents, it was an opportunity for them finally to mourn Tino. They had insisted on naming him, a sign that, despite his early death, they granted him an individual existence. But, until then, they did not suspect the intensity of the pain and guilt they had experienced at his death. As in the case of Mrs. Lemercier discussed at the beginning of this book, the preverbal child pointed out the lack of words that was gnawing away at his parents and that condemned him to a hopeless and relentless search.

There was a strange redundancy here. The cruel event that affected the pregnancy was replicated in the way the child was doomed to run around constantly. Piontelli kept a sharp memory of this and subsequently took great care to note, in her research on fetuses (regardless of whether they were twins), the movements they made. A number of clear findings emerged from her observations, though of course she was dealing with a limited number of cases. In the first place, children are already mobile before birth. Between the ninth and twentieth week of pregnancy, fetuses begin to move their arms and head, to open and close their legs, to suck their thumb, and they even show evidence of a certain sexual activity; these movements are of the same type as those made after birth. Beginning in the eighth week, fetuses also initiate and select these movements in response to stimuli, and these gestures too are identical to those after birth. Nothing changes after birth except the quality and precision of these movements, if only because of the greater force of gravity. In the second place, a twin's movements in utero with respect to its alter ego are apparent and suggest organized behaviors. The general attitudes observed during an ultrasound session are found again after birth: the tendency of one to protect the other, of one to tag along behind his companion, and so on. If, as they say, life begins with the discovery of the other, then twins (or triplets, etc.) are in a privileged position. It does not appear they are more precocious at birth than "normal" newborns. But, although Piontelli cannot prove it for certain, she believes that, in all cases, one can speak of emotional sensitivity and responses, and these may depend in some instances on the mother's state of mind. In the third place, children, particularly twins, replicate in their games, and in their verbal exchanges once they begin to talk, entire pieces of their prenatal life. Between the ages of two and four, these become almost an obsession, as if their present identity depended on these fragments of prenatal life. For Piontelli, this is not a mere reproduction of the past, as a videotape would be, nor is it a compulsive repetition. It is a reconstruction of the past, an effort to link emotions to it and give it a meaning. In short, it is an elaboration, a symbolic advance.

The first thing to take from Piontelli's work, beyond its contribution to the study of repetition, is the idea of the continuity between prenatal and postnatal life. What seems primordial in a psychoanalyst's practice with babies is the need to preserve connections: connections with the mother of course, with the biological father or his "stand-in," connections with society (for example, in the case of adoption), but also connections with the period before birth. The child is born with a sensorial connection to the other that preexists her birth. That is what Dolto taught, what experimental science leads us to believe, and what the observations of Piontelli and others, of whom we will speak later, tend to prove. It is in that respect that, truly, *the baby is a person*. There is a prehistory, even a protohistory of the child, as I argued in an earlier work.[14] Human young are born with a plan whose destiny is more or less thwarted; they live symbolically in a language bath within which they construct themselves. All that is true. Let me summarize matters by saying that the child is already constructed through her many connections and that whether or not she "thrives" depends on whether those connections are preserved.

The Contribution of Haptonomy*

When someone wishes to display a connection to another, even a purely conventional one, she touches him: shakes his hand, kisses him on the cheek or on the lips if she is Russian. It is the skin that makes contact. Touching and coenesthetic (pressure) sensitivity, to be precise, are among the first sensorial qualities to appear in embryogenesis.

Well before she has a functioning auditory system—not until the third trimester of pregnancy—the child can recognize and discriminate the acoustic vibrations reverberating in the amniotic fluid. Haptotherapists sometimes say she "hears through her skin." That "intelligent skin," as Catherine Dolto (daughter of Françoise Dolto) says, allows the fetus, for example, to move toward a known and appreciated voice, such as its father's; to respond to the mother's "internal" invitations (without manual contact); to react to touch, whether it comes from the mother, the father, or the therapist, and whether or not a word accompanies it. The amazing uterine ballet to which touch invites the fetus constitutes a first opening of the body to language.

* Haptonomy, a touch and voice therapy developed by the Dutchman Frans Velman, is used by parents in France to communicate with their baby before and during birth.

The term "intelligent skin" is not simply a manner of speaking; it presupposes a broader vision of the human being. Haptotherapy,[15] as it developed after World War II, took an original approach to the problems of fetal sensoriality, early memory, and the parent-child relationship before birth.

The work haptotherapists do with pregnant women and their fetuses has led to the discovery that every physical, affective, psychic, and emotional event experienced by the mother has immediate repercussions on the child's environment. The child reacts to what "authentically" concerns him. In this, the mother discovers the possibility of an extremely subtle relationship with her child. The father, if the mother invites him to do so, can also enter into contact and establish an "affective" connection with the child, both tactile and vocal. Through the attentions he lavishes on the mother, he will also indirectly include the child in a relationship, and that child will thereby be invited to manifest himself as a desiring subject.

In that three-way relationship (or more, in the case of a multiple pregnancy) established with the aid of a haptotherapist, the child very clearly shows his pleasure or displeasure, his desire for contact, or his need for rest and tranquility. Haptotherapists say that the child, thanks to the "affective confirmation" he receives, develops a basic feeling of security that endures well beyond birth. In return, through his responses, he "confirms his parents affectively," a sign of a very particular dynamic within the parental triad, and between twins. Not only is the child, beginning during intrauterine life, interested in the external world, not only does he react to familiar voices and move closer to them, but he makes his presence felt as a function of the affective context. Although we cannot yet explain it, he even seems to commit to memory the rocking motions he initiates in certain precise circumstances. Here again, there is no fusion between mother and child: recognizing the child as an authentic agent modifies the experience of pregnancy and birth for him and his parents.

Haptotherapy, which conceives of the child as a being in quest of meaning and communication beginning with his intrauterine life, has a preventive aim. For example, it is clear that children "contacted" during pregnancy by haptotherapists are often more alert than the average child after birth. Something on the order of an awakening is sparked in advance by that form of three-way prenatal dialogue. In the case of pathological pregnancies—the illness or death of the child—it allows the parents to be present to the child's pain in a totally different way, merely because he is dislodged from his place as a potential passive victim. Similarly, the child, present through the gestures he echoes, modifies the potential rejection, ambivalence, prohibition, and tragedy that impair the relationship between him and his parents.

Maintaining the Connections

At birth, it is of the utmost importance to maintain "auditory-tactile" contact. This is not always possible because of technology, but it remains necessary. In the aquatic environment, the newborn had the freedom to move toward a sound she perceived; the task is much more arduous in the open air. Of course, observations have shown that a baby, in the first four hours following birth, seeks out the voice of her father, and will manage to turn her head toward him if he speaks to her. And of course, a study in the same laboratory shows that a newborn placed at birth on the belly of her mother cries significantly less than a baby brought directly to her crib, regardless of the attentive care surrounding her. All the same, she is very defenseless.

In fact, in the two examples cited above, the child finds her bearings only through the intermediary of the perception she has of the people she knows, her parents in this instance. We wondered earlier whether the child "before" and "after" birth was the same being, and whether she knew she was; we must now reply yes, provided the sensorial continuum with the mother and her partner is maintained. That is the necessary condition for ensuring that birth is not an act of violence for the child being born.

The midwives of Béclère know that very well. They are intent, once they have observed that everything is going well after the expulsion, on leaving as quickly as possible, if, of course, circumstances and the parents allow it. They are certainly ready to intervene at any moment, but they remain at a distance. They know that these moments following birth belong to the three (or two) protagonists, and that their duty as the medical assistance staff is to not interfere intrusively.

I have also often attended births. I remember, one of the first times I had the opportunity to do so, being struck by the baby's distress when he was separated from his mother to receive routine care. To reduce that distress, I suggested that the father speak to his baby, while at the same time holding his hand to provide an edge, to give him the reassuring boundary of warmth. I then saw the baby turn and seek out his father "by voice," whereas he remained completely insensitive to my voice and to the midwife's. This raised questions in my mind. I have since seen this phenomenon repeated many times.

Do not be too surprised at my sensitivity to the violence of the moments following birth; the most detached professionals have also been known to experience it. The routine care given a newborn can be very aggressive. Whether it entails clearing the nasal cavities or aspirating the remainder of the amniotic fluid and mucus, no gesture is harmless. All the professional tact and competency is needed to "gently" swab the anal, nasal, auricular, and umbilical areas. It takes practice and a sure touch to weigh the child, to measure her, stretching out the limbs still bent as they were in the uterus, and to instill more or less irritating products in the eyes and nose, if these actions are not to be experienced by the child as a series of assaults. Of course, as far as aggression goes, these are relatively benign. But they will have particular repercussions for the child if carried out while she is separated from her mother. Away from her primary source of familiar perception, she has lost any means for reassuring herself.

The baby is seeking the *already known*. I have sometimes advised the mothers I see in the days following birth to place the baby directly against their bare skin, when the connection between them seems to be broken or damaged. Such is the case for women left defenseless by the baby blues. The idea is quite simply that the baby should lie naked on his mother's breast, while she speaks to him if need be. Hence, he remains in contact by touch, hearing, smell, and sight with that other body he already knew and that he now recognizes. That sensorial proximity has a structuring function in that it reactualizes the prenatal connection. But that skin contact, sometimes recommended by the kangaroo unit as well as by me, is desirable only if the mother wishes it. Otherwise, forcing her hand can only be harmful for both protagonists. And why do it? There are so many ways to be a mother, and each should develop her own.

The goal is to maintain the sensory connection between mother and child, and that is often sufficient to protect newborns from the effects of their mother's slight and passing depression. It is also, in more severe cases, the opportunity for the mother to begin to speak of her history, however painful it might be. In any case, maintaining that connection is necessary and beneficial to both.

Through the expansive work of pediatrician Marie Thirion, pediatrics also provides us with a discourse on the mother-child connection. "To live after his birth," Thirion writes, "in an exact resemblance to the very first days after fertilization, when his implantation in the uterus immediately determined his survival or elimination, a newborn must take root in something living, must implant himself in a human relationship."[16] It is a seductive observation and tallies with what I have just said. Thirion adds, "The child, brutally separated from his mother at the time of birth, cut off from her odor, her voice, from her caresses on his body, is unable to *create connections*. . . . When she takes him in her arms, speaking of herself and of him, no longer addressing someone else at the foot of the bed, the child, exhausted, falls asleep. He has created the connection."

A psychoanalyst could put that to her own use, changing only one detail to turn it completely around: It is not a matter of *creating connections* but of *maintaining* them. It is not a matter of a new *attachment,* or of an imprint or connection in ethologist Boris Cyrulnik's sense, but of maintaining and reestablishing a preexisting communication through perceptions and language.

To use a theatrical metaphor, we may say that intrauterine life is a *dress rehearsal*. In attendance are at least the mother as director and a select audience that is part of the company: the father, if he is there, a partner, or close friends and family. The sensorial repertoire is revised, the different voices heard, and the initial plot already brought to a climax. Birth is a *premiere* for an unknown public. No one, not even the "producers," knows how long the venture will last and what success it will have. What is certain is that the proper launch of the play will depend on the connections established during the rehearsals. It remains to be seen how the *newborn* actors hear and speak the lines of the play, how they memorize them, and what "coach" can be useful to them in getting their bearings in cases where problems arise.

3. Speech, Language, and Memory in the Newborn

"Human beings go through their lives like blind people. Words are their white canes." —CHRISTIAN BOBIN

As we saw in the last chapter, conversations with newborns raise provocative questions about repetition. Are prenatal events played out in postnatal situations? Another question raised by conversations with newborns, the most obvious one, is how well the newborn understands us, and we her. Let us avoid the wrong track from the outset: The newborn does not grasp language like someone who has already acquired it. No one, scientist or otherwise, can waste his time thinking that. Nor would anyone believe a therapist who claims that the newborn, though he does not understand the meaning of what she tells him, nevertheless obeys her wish that he feel better in order to humor her.

Speech Addressed to the Newborn

In spite of everything, the psychoanalytic conversation with the newborn has effects on his body. On the psychoanalyst's as well, in fact, since relieving symptoms can energize, whereas complications are exhausting. Dolto had great insight in this matter when she said: "The wound can only be repaired or rather overcome by true words, said by someone the child knows is in agreement with her mother and father, and who speaks to her of the ordeal they have both experienced, she and her mother. . . . Only the word can, in a symbolic manner, reestablish the child's internal cohesion . . . Children, babies, infants understand words, it's astonishing, we don't know how, when they are spoken to them to communicate a truth that concerns them; words that relate what one knows of the facts, without any value judgment."[1]

That is correct: we do not know how, but we know it. One does not have to be a psychoanalyst to observe that mothers and fathers speak to their infants. They willingly attribute a meaning to the different gurgles and babbles of their children, if not to their gestures. If it were only nonsense, the mental health of humanity as a whole would be in danger.

Some might counter that a newborn does not understand language, and that what he perceives of our intervention is, at most, our intentions: the timbre of our voice, the appeal of our smile, the tone we use. Why not? These elements, which linguists call prosodic—accent, tone—combined with the physical constitution of the interlocutors, beginning with their sex, are part of communication. But are there not other signs that suggest that what we do not understand nevertheless exists? It seems we already have several paths of investigation.

The first path is magnetic. Dolto claimed that a child in the preverbal stage can function like magnetic tape. That is, the child is capable of recording phonemes, even words and phrases, which she does not understand in the strict sense.

She knows how to commit them to memory, store them in such a way that these words and phrases can reappear several years later, in circumstances and with a pertinence that are psychologically significant for the child. Let us recall Dolto's discussion of one of her student analysts, a particularly moving case in that it brings together in a single image the beginning and end of a life.

This woman was afflicted with an incurable cancer at the time but, one way or another, was still carrying on with her professional and social life. At what turned out to be her last session, she recounted a dream of inexpressible happiness, which, she said, would have consoled her about everything if it had lasted: "That happiness came from syllables I was hearing [in the dream], meaningless syllables."[2] Within three days, she had become a paraplegic. She died shortly thereafter.

The woman was English and had lived in India between the ages of one month and nine months. She was cared for by a young Indian woman who held her constantly in her arms and rocked her. Their parting, according to what the woman was later told, was heartbreaking. Dolto had an intuition that the incomprehensible syllables in the dream might have been words pronounced by the Indian woman. After an investigation, it turned out it was a sentence that all nannies in that country said to babies: "My little sweetie, whose eyes are more beautiful than the stars." These phonemes, "which had been accompanied by that inexpressible narcissistic pleasure called happiness," served as a last sacrament for the little girl who was losing the nanny who had carried her—losing her legs in some sense. When the words resurfaced later, they foretold the loss of her own legs this time, and her farewell to the world.

From this example we can see that a child who has not acquired any language nevertheless hears, comprehends, and
memorizes bits of semantically and syntactically pertinent
language. *Comprehend* is to be taken in its etymological
sense, "to take with": The child carries a coded message with
her that she cannot decipher, and that message becomes an
integral part of her. In addition, it has effects on her body, un-
beknownst to her. In the case of this woman, it is as if her
body remembered it: She dreams about it. She dreams about
it at a time when, as Dolto says, the same sort of break has occurred in her corporeal system as during the first event. In her
past, it was the moment of seeing herself as an autonomous
body about to start walking. She was going to be separated
from that nanny/body that was, as it were, attached to her,
that walked for her and with her. At present, it was the antic-
ipation of paraplegia and separation from the living world. A
premonitory dream? What is of interest is rather that the
body memorized the enigmatic phrase, that therefore the
body itself is in some sense the place of language. But since
the message is indecipherable as such and the body remembers it nonetheless, the message is coupled with a forgotten—or rather rejected, foreclosed—meaning. The body in
that case is like a palimpsest, a parchment with a text covering the effaced meaning.

IS IT POSSIBLE TO SPEAK OF
A SEMANTICS OF THE NEWBORN?

I have already said that the newborn is sensitive to his
mother's voice. We must go a step farther and seek to know
to what he reacts when he hears it. Marie-Claire Busnel, an

acoustic researcher I mentioned earlier, has for twenty years studied the effect of the mother's voice on her child. In some of her studies, she observed the frequency and variability of heart rates: in the fetus, the newborn, the premature baby. The idea was to interpret these fluctuations as responses to the stimuli of the mother's voice. Without going into detail about her protocols, let us note that she demonstrated at least four fundamental points.

In the first place, the baby recognizes and prefers her mother's voice; she shows that she "hears her" better than she hears other people. In the second place, the baby reacts more when the mother speaks to her than when she speaks to others, in this case, the conductors of the experiment. In the third place, the baby or fetus reacts when the mother thinks of her and communicates with her in thought, though to a lesser degree. In the fourth place—and here an immense field opens for us—not only does the baby react much more to a familiar story or piece of music than to others she hears for the first time, but she displays a greater reaction the more emotionally charged the story is for her or her mother.

We will leave it to the individual to decide whether that means the newborn has a semantics and is endowed with a memory. Busnel herself does not feel authorized to make the leap that would consist of saying that the child's reactions signify she understands in the strict sense. But it is obviously an essential confirmation of what psychoanalysis says.

Furthermore, it is a recommendation for prevention, since Busnel shows that overstimulating the fetus cancels out the hoped-for effect, and can even be harmful to the child. This will disappoint the devotees of frenzied training of babies in early pregnancy. A few musical moments with the fetus will do no damage, of course. But, as Busnel recently recalled, it is an ethical obligation for scientists to say that the systematic application of a learning program for the fetus is abominable and useless.[3]

She illustrated this obligation by recalling the famous experiment on ducks done by the American researcher Gilbert Gottleib. We know that the duckling has a vital need to learn, from gestation on, to recognize its mother's voice. As soon as it emerges from the egg, in fact, it will have to follow her by voice if it does not wish to die. Experimenters thus sought to find out whether, by artificially reproducing, directly in the egg, the stimuli necessary to ducklings for life in the fresh air, they could facilitate the duckling's learning process. They therefore opened the shells and let the fetuses hear the voice of their mothers, while at the same time shining a light in their eyes. The result was catastrophic. The ducklings could not learn anything, as if the two stimuli negated rather than complemented each other. Since vision appears later, it is probable that shining a light in their eyes canceled out the capacity for auditory learning. If the experimenters introduced the two stimuli successively, the ducklings' learning process was very delayed compared to the norm. If they shone light in the eyes without providing the mother's voice, the effect was nil.

Hence we know there is no need to overstimulate "our little ducklings"!

The Newborn's Speech

Almost all neurobiologists now accept the idea that there is no acquisition or memorization possible without "emotive" participation, that is, without the cooperation of the limbic system and the anterior cortex of the cingulum. Some go further and suggest that when one commits a perception to memory, one also memorizes the corresponding emotion. Every piece of stored information is coupled with the emotive information concerning it. That is the gist of neurophysiologist Antonio Damasio's hypothesis of "somatic markers."[4] For Damasio, every decision-making strategy is influenced by general states of the body that inform the brain about the behavior to pursue. These somatic markers function like alarms: for example, when someone salivates at the idea of eating foie gras or gets sick to the stomach imagining a plate of Jerusalem artichokes. The structures that underlie these somatic markers are, on the one hand, the prefrontal cortex, which classifies data concerning the external world and the particular events of every individual's life, and, on the other, the somatosensory cortex, which processes all the kinds of information I dealt with in previous chapters. It is on these structures that our learning about life depends. In other words, to borrow the title of one of Damasio's chapters: No body, no mental representation.

KARINA, OR, FEAR OF LIFE

I have cited these few examples of the connection between language, emotion, and the body because the newborns I happen to hear speak of nothing else. Damasio would probably say they have not yet had time to produce somatic markers, but the bodies of these three-day-old babies send out every sort of alarm: attacks of the respiratory system, troubles with digestion, weight abnormalities, sleep disturbances, anorexia, rejection of the breast, infections—everything is expressed at the site of the body. The language of organs, as they say? Not really. In that case, I would not be able to understand how my words could have a direct effect on these bodily ills.

Karina was a little girl, two days old, hypotonic, who would not eat and whose weight loss was alarming. A midwife even described her as moribund. As for the parents, I was told they were nearly paralyzed, with no reaction other than powerless suffering in the face of their daughter's misfortunes. I went to her bedside.

The mother told me: "You understand, I lost my baby five years ago; it was awful. And now Karina . . ."

This woman had long suffered from infertility, which had finally been overcome after several attempts at in vitro fertilization at Béclère. The resulting child, a boy, died before birth.

"We had everything all set up, don't you see? A cradle, a baby carriage, a car seat, toys. . . . The baptismal gown was ready. What use was it? We threw out all the clothes except what we had borrowed. We had to give the baby carriage to my niece, because at least she's young, she'll be able to have children."

This woman was forty-four years old, and little Karina was her first living baby. She set her up in her bed and, seated in tears beside her, kept vigil as if the child were a corpse. Through her she saw only her dead son; Karina's fate was henceforth connected to that of her elder brother, as if her mother were forbidden to have a child who lived. "So now Karina doesn't want to eat, she's dying before our eyes, it can't be. . . . We're not superstitious, my husband and I, but this time we swore to do everything to see that it wouldn't happen again. We bought practically nothing for her, so as not to tempt fate. Just what was needed, a pair of pajamas, a few baby bottles. Even that was not enough. Now it's clear there's something wrong with her."

The mother, an immigrant, spoke to me of the isolation in which she found herself, and mentioned a plan to go introduce the child to her grandparents, who lived abroad. There was something alive making its appearance there, and I took advantage of it to speak to Karina of the mourning her parents had not performed for the first baby, which seemed to be barring her from taking her place in her family line: "Your parents were so afraid that, like your brother, you wouldn't find a way to live, that they don't know what to do or think. But you're different from your brother and you decided to be born. I don't know if you've decided to live yet. If you want to live, you'll have to eat so you'll get bigger. It's up to you to choose, but know that your parents are ready to do anything to help you."

No reaction from the child. I advised the mother to put Karina directly against her skin to reestablish a connection with her, a connection that seemed as fragile as the faith she had in her daughter's life. I explained to her that Karina could thereby recover the support and security she needed. Then I took my leave.

In the corridor, I found the pediatrician and neonatal nurse who were caring for Karina. The pediatrician considered it a matter of vital urgency to get the child's weight up, and was considering force-feeding her. The nurse proposed bottle-feeding her without the mother present. She added that the mother was doing so poorly that she ran the risk of transmitting her anxiety to her child, cutting off her appetite, so to speak. Both insisted there was no time to waste.

Although I respected the need to intervene quickly, I asked that they wait a few more hours. It seemed to me of the utmost importance that Karina choose on her own to feed herself, and that she settle matters with her mother. To feed Karina away from her mother would run the risk of reinforcing this mother who had such low self-esteem in her feeling of incompetence and would make matters worse.

The pediatrician agreed on a reprieve. Three-quarters of an hour later, Karina had asked for and swallowed nearly two ounces of milk given by her mother. She put on weight in the days that followed, and her parents came to express their relief to me as they were leaving.

MATHIEU, THE LITTLE TATTLETALE

Some will agree with psychoanalyst Serge Lebovici that reading the telephone directory to the baby would have had the same effect. But there was one baby who would have screamed on hearing the directory read out loud. That baby's name was Mathieu.

I met him in the maternity ward, because his mother was distressed about problems awaiting her when she left the hospital. The three of us had a long conversation. In an aside, she explained that she lived in the home of a "gentleman" who lent her two rooms of his apartment in exchange for minor services. He was doing her something of a favor, but obviously that was not without its problems for this woman, problems of practical comfort and privacy. These bouts of kindness were soon to be cut short in any case, since the baby's arrival was less to the taste of the "gentleman" in question.

The discussion changed course, when suddenly she spoke again of the "gentleman," but this time by name "Mr. X." At that point, Mathieu screamed. When, at the end of the conversation, his mother murmured to me: "In confidence, I can tell you, but don't repeat it: Mr. X is Mathieu's father," I had no trouble replying that I had understood as much, because Mathieu had already pointed it out to me. Coincidence?

In any case, he reacted like a man to that psychoanalytic commonplace of recent years, that it is up to the mother to name the father to the child's ears. From that moment on, the name of the father was no longer a vacant place for Mathieu. If one or the other of the parents felt ill at ease, let us wager that Mathieu's unconscious, through a typical case of infantile amnesia, for example, might later modestly veil the statue. Some will say that the only circumstances under which it may be useful to talk to the baby is when one seeks indirectly to reach his parents, who would have trouble tolerating certain things if they were said bluntly. This is an elegant and clever remark, and, in certain cases, one acts accordingly. But is it not disrespectful to embrace that "ruse"? Disrespectful, not to the parents or the baby, but to the truth?

As soon as possible, it is better to render unto Caesar what is Caesar's: If the parents are the center of the problem, one must speak to the parents. If it's the child, then address him. After all, he's the patient.

MAURICE AND THE MARABOUT

Conversely, I sometimes speak to a mother so that her child will hear. That is the case for premature babies and was true for Marie Perrier, the baby with jaundice whom I have already mentioned. I speak to the child's mother because I am unable to address her directly, in the hope that it will have an effect. I may also address the mother or father in the baby's presence, as in the obvious case where the solution depends on them. That was the case for Maurice.

Maurice, six days old, had a weight problem as well. For him, it was that, already, he could not manage to stay trim. I say that with a smile, but his weight gain was a threat to him. No one understood why he was swelling up like the frog in the fable who wanted to be as big as an ox, not the members of the staff or his parents. He was the fifth child, born of extremely jovial parents, with a mother so tender and attentive that you could hardly dare imagine such a one. But the marabout, or Muslim holy man, whom his parents had voluntarily consulted during the pregnancy had singled him out as "different." That pronouncement on the child's fate had left the father in a state of panic. He spoke to us in a very calm voice of the terrifying nightmares he had had recently about the child, which had the immediate effect of waking Maurice with a start and making him cry out. (At least this child understood his father if he did not understand me. Another coincidence, no doubt, which made him react with fear at the familiar voice of a father who spoke in all serenity of the most horrible dreams.) The mother shared her husband's anxiety in another form, as I realized during the conversation. As soon as the baby made any move whatever, she became frightened, thinking of his troubling "difference." Then, systematically, she offered him the breast. In fact, as she told me, she had been practicing the same strategy for a week, to "calm" him. Hence the weight gain. In believing she was "calming" *him,* she was reassuring herself. Since Maurice was a generous fellow and an intelligent son, he suckled readily, thus assuring his mother he was not at all afraid of his father's nightmares, but that, as she imagined, he was hungry. In any case, when I in turn reassured the parents, explaining to them that he might be "different" in the future, but that for the moment it was their job to protect him and not the reverse, he no longer got quite so hungry, it seems. In the two days that followed, things settled down and Maurice's weight gain returned to a normal rate.

THE NEWBORN'S APTITUDE FOR LANGUAGE

To acquire language is one thing, to have the aptitude to do so is another, just as understanding a language is one thing, speaking it another. On these two points, psychoanalysis and neurobiology are in agreement: The human baby has not acquired language, but already has in place mechanisms that allow him to do so, unlike other primate babies. That, at least, is the viewpoint of a group of the most important and innovative neuroscientists. In a recent work,[5] Gerald M. Edelman presents theses on language that, though they may seem daunting at first glance for a nonspecialist, provide the pleasure of discovering something new.

Let me give a brief summary of his work. If we are to speak and understand a language, and to construct a language within us, at least two phases are required, he says. First, we must have what he calls a primary consciousness of things; that is, we must be capable of arranging our perceptions into a series, as a function of our past experiences and the "costs" they entailed (satisfaction or displeasure). This means reacting to the information about the present that reality would like to present to us, and sifting it through our memory. Without that ability, speaking becomes problematic. Let me cite in that respect an example of what is called "blindsight" (visual anosognosia). Blindsight is caused by a lesion on the primary visual cortex; a person with this condition still sees perfectly well, but says he cannot see. For example, he can pick up a fork and use it as it ought to be used, but if someone asks him what is located on the table in front of him, he will reply: "I don't see anything." That primary consciousness introduces a first perceptive "bootstrapping" between two types of nerve structures: the limbic system and the cerebral trunk, which slowly process information as a function of the pleasure experienced; and the thalamocortical system, which rapidly analyzes what it can learn of the new situation. Up to this point, there is nothing too complicated, and, after all, in this respect we differ little from our cousins the chimpanzees. In that system, we are under the sole sway of the tyranny of experiences of the present, and are limited in our perspective.

The second phase consists of what Edelman calls a

higher-order consciousness, which is supposedly the primary characteristic of humans, and hence intimately connected to language. It consists, thanks to language, of appropriating for ourselves the sensations to which our primary consciousness has granted a particular value, of "embodying" them. I mentioned before the "noses" in the perfume business; one might also mention wine tasters. According to Edelman, their talent can be considered the result of a passion founded on sensations which become increasingly refined thanks to language. From the neurophysiologic point of view, that higher-order consciousness is the result of a second, semantic bootstrapping between the cortical regions of language, by means of which words and phrases, their resonance, significance, and syntax are developed and memorized, and the prefrontal cortex responsible for classifying ideas. In fact, to speak one must emit not only sounds, but sounds related to ideas that have a meaning. The interesting thing is that Edelman makes these capacities the equivalent of a "symbolic memory." That is, one does not speak only because one wants to say something, one speaks because one is inventing, because one is inventing while speaking, and because one speaks of oneself confronting the world while speaking of rain and fair weather. Obviously, that perspective delights the psychoanalyst, because, beyond the explanation it provides of brain functions, it draws attention to the singularity of the individual. Creativity in language is a personal matter. It is the act of every being faced with the questions that haunt one's life; it is one's fragrance, one might say. As a psychoanalyst, I am only remotely interested in whether speech is an *acquired* competency (under the influence of the community to which one belongs) or whether the mechanism for acquiring language is *innate*. It is more important to be able to say that language, like sensation, is constructed with the other person, and to add, thanks to my practice with babies, that that construction occurs earlier than the appearance of spoken language itself. Edelman claims that the attribution of meaning to symbols is not carried out formally; symbolic structures have a meaning from the outset. The idealized cognitive models appeal to conceptual embodiment and the latter comes about thanks to corporeal activities prior to language.

It is particularly interesting to hear Edelman explain that when the symbols used do not correspond directly to what exists in the world, human beings use metaphors and metonymies to establish connections. This intersects with an entire aspect of psychoanalytic theory related to the themes of condensation and displacement in dreams, which others have translated in terms of metaphor and metonymy. This is not the place to repeat them, except to cite Lacan's bon mot regarding the creativity of language. If metaphor consists of taking one word for another, then children's errors are creative: "The cat goes bow wow, the dog goes meow meow. . . . That is how the child spells out the powers of discourse and inaugurates thought."[6]

Day Four: The Moment to Make Oneself Heard

Hence, the human brain may be programmed for speech, or at least programmed to emit sounds. A baby, in the maternity ward as elsewhere, gurgles, screams, cries, smiles. Is that a language, however? In any case, we cannot reject the evidence that it is an effort at communication. Of course, daily dealings with babies show it is not a targeted communication like theater dialogue. It is rather like throwing a stone into a pond, calling high and low: greetings to one and all!

In the maternity ward, the first thing you hear is crying, obviously, since that is newborns' favorite vocal mode of expression. Sometimes the noise level or tear level crosses the tolerance threshold of adults, and I am asked to intervene. I remember being able to interpret the reasons a four-day-old baby was crying, which he had been doing continually since his birth. One of the night nurses told me she had not heard him cry since I'd spoken to him. She added: "If I'd known, I would have pointed him out before; that would have spared me three exhausting nights!" The baby as well no doubt. The fact that the nurse singled out that child proves that she knew the child was saying something, and that a psychoanalyst might perhaps understand him.

You also hear exclamations and words of joy on the ward, like those of the obstetrician who jumped up and down in the corridors next to the labor rooms, in surgeon's scrubs and clogs, leaping and shouting between gasps that she "had delivered a baby the way she liked." More generally, a maternity ward sometimes resembles a rehearsal hall, where all the musicians are tuning up before the concert; they clear their throats or rosin their bows, tune their instruments, do their scales, test their voices, all completely independent of those around them.

In addition, there is screaming in the maternity rooms. In the best of cases, there is the babbling of babies. That is common, moreover, and energizes everyone. It is not harmless. It is even one of the paths we must follow to use language, in keeping with Dolto's hypothesis of chronological repetition and the hypotheses of neuroscience. If we are to pay heed to Boris Cyrulnik, an ethologist specializing in human behavior, screaming and babbling are the first seeds of speech. The proof? Cyrulnik recorded the screams of newborns, which he studied with a machine that analyzes frequency. He noticed that the histograms (graphs representing different vocal frequencies) of these screams had different shapes depending on whether the newborns were "among themselves," "responding" to one another from crib to crib, or whether adults were among them speaking to one another. In short, in one case it was cacophony, in the other, beginning on day four, it assumed a clearly melodic aspect.[7] The experiment was conclusive. It proved that, like the sensations I mentioned earlier, speech (of one, the baby) needs speech (of the other, the adult, or the baby's twin or another baby).

Such an argument allowed me to better understand the baby blues, which, as we know, appear on about the third or fourth day. During the first days, it is as if the only sounds the babies make are screams, merely phonic echoes of their condition: a cold and realistic discourse in short. They scream to assert their want: "I'm hungry," "I'm cold," "I'm sleepy and it's too noisy," or "I'm uncomfortable," "I've got a stomachache." These are simple assertions of what they are feeling, a sort of psalmody that translates their sensations. Then, all of a sudden, another private and delicate mechanism is set in place between mother and child, because the child realizes the mother is the one who supplies his needs. A new sort of language modulation can be heard, which varies as a function of the mother and is addressed to her.

If that new vocal communication fails, because, for example, the mother is too depressed, the newborn may resort to a symptom. In the place of tears, for example, there will be colic, spitting up, or vomiting. At that moment, in fact, a regular game of Ping-Pong can set in between the child and the mother, as pediatricians well know.

That was the case for a woman whose two children suffered from colic. She found their poor digestion so unbearable that feeding time was becoming a torment for her. She was anxious because they had stomachaches, and we may easily suppose that, in return, they had stomachaches as a result of feeling their mother's anxiety; it was like a bottomless pit. After three or four months, happily, their digestive system matured; on their own, they found another way of functioning, stopped spitting up and being sick to their stomachs, and everything became normal. In fact, the mother felt guilty that she had not breastfed them, and blamed the infant formula for her children's colic. This argument is fallacious since commercial infant formula is now extremely well tolerated. But, for her, that was the true reason. Then one day, her father, seeing her getting worked up because of the stomach distress of her second son, whom she was bottle-feeding, innocently let it slip out: "It's just like with you, in the end; they take after you."

"What do you mean? I was breastfed!"

"That's true, but you had a stomachache all the time. No one knew how to comfort you at first, not me or your mother. I remember we took turns pacing with you all night long to calm you down!"

She began to think that, all the same, you could be a good mother even if you bottle-fed the baby. This woman was, as it were, relieved by that thought. Her children to come will be more at ease; perhaps they will have fewer stomachaches, or perhaps she will give herself permission to breastfeed them.

The Language Bath and the First Smile

What about smiling? Oh, the beauty of the first smile. . . . Well, no, according to Cyrulnik, it's an optical illusion. The first smile is the result of a secretion of a neuropeptide, and the mother misinterprets it when she sees it as payment to her. But let us follow Cyrulnik further. He takes the counterexample of the baby blues, that is, of depressed women who remain impassive when their babies smile. They create around the babies what he calls a "cold sensorial world" and thereby compromise the babies' sleep, and hence their future growth.

That is certainly a risk in serious depression, but one does not see it in the classic case of baby blues, the normal if not necessary depression that affects the majority of new mothers to one degree or another. On the contrary, these mothers' lassitude—"I don't know how to take care of him, I'll never manage"—their slight depression, seems to be a *necessary* appeal to the child to act like a human being. For his part, his response will mark the beginning of oral communication.

This thesis needs to be supported by clinical examples and, out of concern for clarity, I shall put off giving a more detailed explanation until chapter 5, which is devoted to "limbo." Beyond this slight disagreement with Cyrulnik, I too am persuaded of the need for the language bath, which is demonstrated every day in the maternity ward. Perhaps

Cyrulnik will judge me faithful in that respect to what he articulates later on: "Not only are neurological prerequisites necessary for access to language to be opened, but affective prerequisites are also necessary. The behavioral system that *supports* speech and makes it come to pass presupposes, around the child, the presence of some other being to talk to, to talk for; another word must respond to one's own."[8] Cyrulnik demonstrates the existence of that language bath in terms of the process of designation, which he believes is the precondition for acceding to symbolism and language. Unlike other primates, in fact, human beings *spontaneously* learn to point their fingers to designate an object, and they understand when another person is pointing to something. They acquire that skill at about a year old, according to Cyrulnik's observations. These observations were videotaped, and, in viewing these tapes, he noted that the appearance of finger pointing in a child is invariably accompanied by another behavior: The child begins to look at the parent or adult who is with her during the "experiment" and attempts to pronounce a word addressed to him or her. That is why the ethologist can say that "language . . . takes its place not in a face-to-face relationship between the child and the thing she designates, but by virtue of a double affective reference to the thing and to the person to whom she is attached."[9]

The Aptitude to Form Syllables

Let us add a few words on the communication *by* and *with* the infant. I borrow from the neurologist and aphasiologist Gisèle Gelbert, whose theories opened a new, extraordinarily effective clinical approach to language difficulties.

For Gelbert, it is because someone speaks to the child that he will himself speak. In the beginning was the word? No, in the beginning was the thought, supported by that "structure carried by the child before any external word."[10] The human brain is programmed for speech; the child has an "aptitude to form syllables." But a step intervenes between hearing or discriminating sounds and reproducing them, and another step between reproducing and creating sounds. According to Gelbert, it is the appearance of "external oral propositions" (from the mother, for example) that will allow the child to have "oral propositions of his own." The speech the child hears "will be simultaneously listened to and analyzed." The language heard will become *his* language.

Gelbert chooses to exclude from her demonstration any psychoaffective (relating to the mind's response to emotions) context, preferring to rely on others to provide it. Psychoanalysts will say there is no psychic aspect without an affective aspect, and that the latter structures the former. Let us retain from the neurologist's arguments that the child speaks because someone spoke to him. This is not merely a truism, since it implies, on the one hand, that the so-called mother tongue is constructed *with* the mother after birth, and, on the other, that this mother tongue relies on the psychic, which exists *before* birth.

On this problem of newborns' "language," it is clear that the field is still wide open. In attempts at scientific explanation, one sees fairly well the uncertainty remaining about what newborns "understand" and what they "say." In what language do they speak? We do not know. We know they do not understand in the linguistic sense of the term: Their semantics, their phonetics, and their syntax are not our own. Conversely, clinical experience, supported by the process of listening psychoanalytically, provides the certainty that they "understand" and that they "say." How do they speak? In the original language, their unique language, without subtitles. The only way to prove this is by giving an account of that clinical experience, attempting to give a glimpse of the emotion a psychoanalyst may feel when a child addresses or responds to one or another of her interventions. It would be presumptuous to make any further claims; it would run the risk of falling into a "very dangerous state: that of believing one understands,"[11] as the writer Paul Valéry said. "The clear mind makes it understood what it does not understand," he added. We must attempt to embrace that ideal, to learn our lessons, one way or another, from newborns in distress. Indeed, what do these babies do, if not attempt to make it understood to anyone who will hear them what they do not understand and what is affecting their bodies?

Memory

Gerald Edelman spoke of "primary consciousness" and "higher-order consciousness." What of the unconscious in all that? Curiously, at the present time, it is researchers interested in memory who are taking the unconscious into account. There is nothing astonishing about that in the end, if one begins from the principle that everything we have spoken of heretofore, namely, fetal and infant sensoriality, repetition, and language, has memory as a common precondition.

The psychiatrist Daniel Stern, one of the pioneers in the observation of infants, reminds us that, for the infant, memory guarantees the *permanence of self;* it gives the newborn a sense of wanting to "continue to be," as Winnicott said. Although the clinical conclusions Stern draws from his hypotheses have not always met with unanimous agreement, this new development is particularly interesting. For him, memory is constructed with the other, following the modalities of what he calls *representations of interactions that have been generalized* (RIGs). With his mother, the baby learns to distinguish, to categorize, and to memorize "*specific episodes* of life-as-lived (for example, 'that one time when Mommy put me to bed to go to sleep, but she was distraught and only going through the motions of the bedtime ritual and I was overtired, and she couldn't help me push through that familiar barrier into sleep') and *generalized episodes* ('what happens when Mommy puts me down to sleep')."[12] As a result, the basis of memory is affective as much as perceptive. It really seems that neurobiology is now reaching the point of demonstrating that thesis.

A CREATIVE MEMORY

What sort of memory are we speaking of? A very singular memory, faithful and inaccurate at once, human. Hence there are events in general one does not forget, like the deaths of those close to us. Newborns also do not forget. I cited the infant treated by Piontelli who was looking everywhere for his twin who had died in utero. Unfortunately, I have seen many similar cases at Béclère, where the number of pregnancies of twins or triplets is far higher than average. Of the twins to whom that tragedy has occurred and who are singled out because they cry too much, because they do not eat, or because their mother is depressed, practically all recover their equilibrium when I speak with them and their parents about the mourning to be performed for their lost brother or sister.

It has reached the point that I can make it grounds for systematic prevention, as with premature births and separations from the mother. In addition, in thorny situations such as these, midwives come to me on their own and say: "Mrs. X had a child whose twin died a month before term. He cries all the time. What should we do?" or "That lady was pregnant with triplets, but one of the three died."

In general, parents on their own inform their baby of the pain they have to face. Nevertheless, it sometimes happens that a symptom signals to us that they may need an extra nudge.

Once more, that nudge consists of talking to the newborns. Why speak to them? Because, once more, it is a way of bridging the gap between the sensations of these children, who we know have experienced the death of their companion in the womb, and their suffering, which is something like a desperate echo of it after birth. Perinatal mourning is always to be taken into consideration.

In fact, it is as if these newborns are remembering the event *wrong*, but not *mistakenly*. Wrong, because their symptoms can seem senseless, with no "reasonable" limit. But rightly, in the sense that the postnatal sorrow from which these symptoms originate is perfectly justified. If we take as an example the extreme case of newborns who not only remember grief, but a grief that is not their own, it will be clear why I speak of remembering *wrong* but not *mistakenly*.

The Lady in Black

There was a woman who experienced the sorrow of losing her sister, and then, during her pregnancy, her mother. Let us call her the lady in black, since in bed after her delivery, she still seemed draped in a horrible shroud. "Thrift, thrift!" For her as for Hamlet, "the funeral bak'd meats did coldly furnish forth the marriage tables." The woman was extremely sad, but she tried to put on a brave face for her child. The relation she established between the death and the birth was her sorrow that her mother could not see her granddaughter, Eva. The child cried as well, terrible, guttural, unbearable cries. I am an opera fan, and I heard in it the grain of voice that makes a cry become sorrow incarnate. She was crying from pain, not from lack of sleep or food or attention or consolation: This pain was beyond lack and need. I mention opera because her screams were public. She had practically drowned out the meeting with the new mothers we had that day. She cried continuously during the meeting, and her audience, far from being annoyed, was overcome by the pain the child was intoning.

It is said that a newborn's cries make her mother's milk come in.[13] I will give my opinion on that question later. In any case, during the conversation she had with me, the lady in black complained she did not have any milk, and saw that as the reason for her baby's screams. In fact, the child was not really dying of hunger, and that is why the staff hesitated to give her a substitute for mother's milk, for fear that such an action would keep the mother's milk from coming in. There was a slight delay, in fact; but to infer from this that she was starving her child, as the woman thought, was unwarranted. The milk came in within two hours of our conversation, which of course corresponded to the length of time expected, but suggests that the conversation had a cathartic effect.

In addition, the more sensitive this woman was to her

child's cries, the more powerless she felt. As a result, she believed the child inconsolable when it was she who was. As I said, her mother had died while the woman was pregnant. Her relationship with her mother had always been difficult, and if ever there was motherly tenderness in the family, it came from the lady in black herself, since she cared for her sister as if she were her daughter. Nevertheless, when the lady in black got pregnant, her mother had become closer to her. In a moment of tenderness as she had never known, the mother confided that she was sure the woman would make a good mother. She supported her, backed her up, assisted her, as she had never done before. As the lady in black said: "I finally had a mother!" It was that new mother the lady in black was mourning: the mother whom she had finally found and immediately lost, the mother who assured her of her confidence in the daughter. In losing her, the woman also lost the self-assurance that she could be a "good mother," or even that she would have enough milk to feed her child. She imagined her baby was paying the price.

I do not think the baby was paying anything; she was keeping score. She had recorded her mother's changes and stress at the news of her grandmother's death, had committed them to memory and was also grieving that death, but without really knowing why. Her mother was so overwhelmed with grief, had so much trouble giving life to her, that she had not taken the time to speak to her. The child was crying because she believed she was the cause of her mother's sorrow. Since she felt incapable of consoling her, the child cried all the more. That was a way of keeping her mother "occupied." It was that vicious circle I had to break, by telling the baby that she might well remember the pain experienced by her mother during pregnancy, but that she was not responsible for it; and the mother, that her own mother's death was not a bad omen that would make her a mother incapable of feeding her child. That was not much, but it was enough. The child's cries ceased, and, when the milk came in within the following hours, it finally reassured the lady in black and her child.

THE MEMORIZATION PROCESS

In order to understand more fully how the lady in black's baby misunderstood her mother's sorrow, let us look at the brain and its memory.

First point: No human being has the same brain as another, not even his twin. As Israel Rosenfield, M.D., explains in *The Invention of Memory*,[14] the differentiation of cells during embryonic development is not merely the application of a genetic program. Whether a cell becomes a neuron, a liver cell, or a skin cell also depends on the location of these cells and their movement during embryogenesis. There is no great gene architect who designed the cerebral organizational system in advance. We are dealing with pieces that fall into place, move, adjust themselves in relation to one another. These "pieces" are groups of cells connected by a cement Edelman calls CAMs, cell adhesion molecules. For example, the specific N-CAMs of neurons will merge with other N-CAMs, taking great care not to fall in with the specific CAMS of liver or skin cells: to each its own territory. It is these CAMs that define the extent to which the different groups join together or stand apart. Hence, on one side is a genetic background that guarantees a family resemblance among all human brains. Building on this background, the CAMs, as a function of cellular topology and of their rambling journey, are the bulwark of individual variations. And these variations are largely dependent on the context.

Second point: The system of neuronal organization is in place during embryogenesis; only the degree of connection will change after birth, as a function of external stimuli. These variations, according to Edelman and Rosenfield, culminate in true neuron maps, themselves composed of neuron subgroups as defined above.

Third point: Within that system, memory is not, strictly speaking, a localized process. To be sure, memories must be stored somewhere in the brain, but why is it so difficult for us to retrieve them? It seems that, since neuropsychologist David Marr's studies, memory can be considered an inventive process. This means that, like magicians, we reinvent our past. Or, to cite the English psychologist Frederic Bartlett quoted by Rosenfield: "Remembering is not the re-excitation of innumerable fixed, lifeless and fragmentary traces. It is an imaginative reconstruction, or construction, built out of the relation of our attitude towards a whole active mass of organized past reactions of experience, and to a little outstanding detail which commonly appears in image or in language form. It is thus hardly ever really exact, even in the most rudimentary cases of rote recapitulation, and it is not at all important that it should be so."[15]

Memory is rarely faithful. For those who might doubt this, let us take the example of dreams, which no one will dispute have to do with recollections, but which deform them at the very least. Beginning in the second half of pregnancy, the fetus dreams. We may even say that, for it, to memorize

is to dream. It feeds its dreams with the information perceived during its rare waking hours, and its dreams serve in
some sense to interpret these sensorial data, and to store them
away at its own convenience. That, for Cyrulnik, is what
marks the birth of intrauterine psychic life.[16] But how does it
store its information *through* the dream? This is particularly
important to know in that, for the moment, neurophysiologists can explain only short-term memory, or, let us say, what
is retained between a few minutes and three days. Yet the
dream is the place where recollections become "stabilized" so
that they can be retained long-term.

The most daring hypothesis about the memory process
contends that the information to be memorized takes two
principal highways. It moves first through a somatosensorial
circuit, which, to reach the primary perception areas of the
brain (the visual and auditory areas, for example), passes
through the cloverleaf of the thalamus, which distributes
different perceptual data to the cerebral areas capable of processing them. That is the highway that has to be taken to get
to memorization, and like a busy highway, it is fairly con-
gested. By itself, it represents close to 99 percent of the traffic
of information to be memorized. In spite of that, all that
information tries to go fast. Travel time from one end of
the chain to the other via the neuron synapses is less than
three hundred milliseconds. That is the rapid information-
processing circuit.

Parallel to it, information takes a second, neurovegetative
circuit whose central axis is the hypothalamus, which places
the prefrontal cortex (site of Edelman's "higher-order consciousness") in contact with the limbic system ("seat of the
emotions"). That secondary axis is much less traveled, and

the speed limit is better respected. It represents only 1 percent of the total traffic, and the travel time for information is greater than four hundred or even five hundred milliseconds. This is the slow information-processing circuit.

Therein lies the crux of the problem. As it happens, this second axis, though apparently minor, is decisive. Let us imagine we are on a busy freeway and that we are perpetually being followed on a side road by a unit of the highway patrol, which forces us to slow down when we get going too fast. That is what happens with this slow information-processing circuit. By means of an enzymatic, and no longer electric, modification, this "patrol unit" controls the speed of the rapid information traffic, and can give the order to change roads and to slow down. Then it disappears, allowing the information to come back onto the main highway. This game of "stop, or else!" is regulated by the monoamine-modulating neurons (the neurons that deliver dopamine, serotonin, or norepinephrine), those that have attracted attention for the role they play in Parkinson's disease, and whose modulating function many psychotropic drugs put to use. These neurons are responsible for slowing down the information, or rather, for extracting information from the first circuit to record it more securely. It is as if the highway patrol invited us to go back and drive over the road a second time at a slower speed, to give us time to reflect. For a more precise and less metaphoric explanation of these phenomena, see the articles by Jean-Pol Tassin, a neuropharmacologist at the Collège de France and the author of studies on this question.[17] The words of an artist, the novelist Pascal Quignard in this case, echo the scientist's discourse: "It so happens that the difficulty presented by the function of memory is not that of storing what has been imprinted in the body's matter. It is that of selecting, setting apart, recalling, and bringing forth again a unique element within what was stored as a single mass. Forgetting is not amnesia. Forgetting is a refusal to bring back to mind part of the mass of the past."[18] As Freud already said, the artist always precedes the scientist in the revelation of the psyche.

Dream Memory

A good illustration of the role of neuromodulators lies in sleep. When a person falls asleep, there is a relative inhibition of the neuromodulators, but dreams represent the moment when they are intensely, but briefly, reactivated.

Since the 1970s, neurobiologist Michel Jouvet's studies on dreaming have interested the scientific community as much as the general public. Jouvet has shown the correlation between a phase of electrical brain activity he has called "paradoxical sleep" and dreaming. Since the people he awakened from paradoxical sleep recounted a dream, he concluded that paradoxical sleep was central to dreaming. Since then, a further step has been taken. Scientists have shown, in effect, that there are phases of "microwaking" during slow sleep, that is, between the different phases of paradoxical sleep. These periods of microwaking correspond to a moment when the neuromodulators, which had been at rest until then, are suddenly activated. All information up to that point was the object of rapid processing during sleep, and, all of a sudden, the neuromodulators transfer it to slow processing. Suddenly, the brain, coming to a waking and conscious state, slows down the information and produces a dream in three hundred milliseconds, even if it takes a half-hour to recount it. It is this "slow" system of rendering information coherent that makes it possible to organize the narrative. To state things bluntly, let us assert with Tassin that it is because one is awakened that one dreams.

The Attracting Fields of Memory

Let us resume our journey. Rapid information processing can be called *analogical*. It consists of selecting similar salient elements and committing them to memory in the form of *attracting fields*. These fields "attract" to themselves every new perceptual element similar to the elements that constitute the memory. They compare these elements immediately to their storehouse. Once that verification is completed, the new element is identified by extrapolation to the overall form known. Hence, when we recognize a face at a glance, it is because we have unconsciously identified three or four salient elements of the face. Then, on the basis of these few elements, we instantly reconstitute the face. Similarly, the infant recognizes his mother's face, whether it is smiling or sad, tense or relaxed. He can also recognize the profile of a face he has seen only in three-quarters profile. That processing is rapid, and is a source of errors for that reason. If we are presented with two faces that, though different, have the same salient characteristics, we may mix up the two, provided they are not very familiar to us. Both will be attracted to the same field and will be confused. If we are presented with a checkerboard with one white square blackened in, we will "recognize" the checkerboard all the same, without being disturbed by that little difference. On the contrary, slow processing is a *cognitive*, logical processing. In the example of the checkerboard, it will allow us to keep the checkerboard in our memory, then to observe, analyzing each of the elements, that there is one square that is now black.

In Tassin's view, rapid processing, or at least the ever-changing balance between rapid and slow processing, can be assimilated to the neurobiological foundation of what Freud called the unconscious. Who knows? This hypothesis is courageous coming from a high-level scientist. He adds that the fetus and the child, before acquiring language, have for the most part access only to rapid processing, primarily because of the immaturity of their prefrontal cortex; slow processing appears later, parallel to cognitive development.

Is it possible, however, that in speaking to babies during the postpartum period, we deliver slow processing to them "ready made," given that they cannot manufacture it on their own? That is the hypothesis put forth by Tassin to explain clinical observations. Nothing in his theses seems to run counter to the claim that the newborn can process analogically a cognitive piece of information given her, and can later find herself equipped to reprocess it herself cognitively. I leave it to the wisdom of scientists to verify experimentally the veracity of that thesis.

Extracting and Slowing Down Information

What does it mean to commit something to memory? For Tassin, it means *extracting* information from rapid processing to *slow it down*. He asserts, however, that slowing down information does not allow it to be stored. Every time one has access to something, one can analyze it, but it must later be

stored analogically. Cognitive processing will therefore modify its own analogical storehouse, and will favor the emergence of new attracting fields. Paradoxically, then, at that
moment there will be both "rapid" and "slow" events, cognitive elements in the analogical storehouse. For Tassin, this information, which has gone through cognitive processing and
been stored again analogically, constitutes the psychoanalytic
unconscious. Theoretically, one can have access to it and can
reactivate it, unless certain painful, or overly pleasurable, elements are incorporated into it. In that case, repression or denial occurs. It is a necessary repression, moreover, because,
without repression, one enters the hell of hypermnesia. Consider the patient described by neuropsychologist Alexander
Luria, who could forget absolutely nothing of what he experienced: Tethered to the auditory and visual memories of his
early years, he was totally incapable of living in the present,
or of making plans for the future.

Infantile Amnesia

It seems extremely difficult to recall memories of earliest
childhood. Everyone has been struck by the poorly explained
phenomenon of infantile amnesia. Some people who have
been through psychoanalysis, however, have claimed that
they recovered key memories from their first two years. In
addition, people who have awakened from comas or been
revived after "dying" say they saw images stream past. Neurophysiologists retort that these are at best screen memories, at worst, imaginary constructions. Tassin says nearly
the same thing: One cannot reactivate consciously—that is,
via slow/cognitive processing—early systems that were pro-

cessed only rapidly/analogically, because the salient elements retained for mnemonic discrimination were too simple.

Consequently, a newborn, who works only analogically, cannot "slow down" his processing in the sense that he is not capable of sharing it. In other words, he does not know how to speak. He is a closed loop. As a result, how are we to interpret, say, the cries of the daughter of the lady in black? How are we to understand Piontelli's assurance that, in her observations, repressed prenatal emotions nonetheless still have an effect beyond infantile amnesia?

As we said, Piontelli complemented her prenatal investigations during ultrasounds with interviews with the same children in the five years following their birth. For her, everything demonstrates that children between two and four years old reproduce their prenatal past through their play. Everyone will easily agree that human young are social animals, as their play demonstrates. As Stern says, for the infant, the other is "an other that regulates the self"; it is through the other that the child constructs her subjectivity. But, in replaying their prenatal past, the children Piontelli discusses seek to give it a meaning and to express the emotions connected to it. They do not simply repeat that past, they elaborate on it. She cites the drawing a boy named Fabrizio made of a pillow with a mouth and two eyes, and that he commented on as follows: "Pillows move. I've never had any peace, not even at night." The allusion was transparent for anyone familiar with his intrauterine life, since, as it happens, he shared an amniotic sac with his twin, Giorgio. One of the consequences of that peculiarity was that, in effect, his brother was his pillow, with a mouth and two eyes, and this pillow moved continuously.

When children are about four and a half years old, infantile amnesia takes effect. At that point, it seems, the children's play or stories still reflect prenatal experiences, but in a roundabout way, without their ever being conscious of it. Rather, stories and games are myths that combine prenatal memories—reduced to slips of the tongue or symptomatic acts—and projections of the children's present life. Take the example of Marisa and Béatrice, twins who had the habit of fighting, both before and after birth. After age five, they no longer allowed the memories of their ancestral battle to surface, except in the form of drawings, and, even then, without seeming to touch on it. One twin depicted her house, scrupulously inscribing all the names of members of her family, except, of course, her twin's. The other drew a house on which she inscribed "away from home!" and another house she said was hers, explaining that it could contain no more than one child.

Piontelli concluded that early if not prenatal memories rediscovered by adults in analysis stem more from reconstructions than from historical reality. In her love of rigor, however, she has placed her hope in the refinement of ultrasound technology to understand these memories better.

I too believe that if there is prenatal trauma, it remains unconscious. If an unexpressed memory—an analogical memory, so to speak—exists in the newborn, it must be able to find expression: by the parents and grandparents or friends if possible; by the psychoanalyst if that expression is forbidden. The role of a psychoanalyst who works with newborns is to name that memory if it has not been named, to put speech in the place where there was only an unexpressed meaning, a "hole of language." The words spoken to the child, or the interpretation given the child of the contents of his parents' unconscious that keep him from thriving, can be justified in that they liberate something that remained wedged inside the postnatal symptom.

We all suffer from a lack of words. When they turn up missing, they can be found in history. History, for its part, needs to be told to someone, by its protagonists if possible. Even before thinking about talking to babies in a psychoanalytic context, we must prepare a space so that that history can be told to another, in this case the psychoanalyst. In that sense, there is not necessarily a need for interpretation. The psychoanalyst's presence can sometimes be enough to allow words to come fill the holes of language, words on the mother's part, for example. But that will be possible only through a mechanism that guarantees that possibility: psychoanalytic sessions.

4. *Doing Psychoanalysis on a Maternity Ward*

"The most intimate confidences are sometimes made to people who pass like shadows, whom one never forgets." —KLEBER HAEDENS

A male midwife had me called in one day during a delivery.

The labor had lasted so long that he thought a mental block was preventing the mother from delivering. I was busy at the time and arrived only at the moment of expulsion, which was going badly. After the conventional greetings, I immediately addressed the mother: "Hello, I've come to help you welcome your baby the best I can." She looked at me wide-eyed—and gave birth at once.

It is said that women seeking to be treated for infertility can become pregnant the same day they meet the senior consultant at the hospital. This is even the subject of off-color jokes in our profession. All the same, what a sudden change of course! I am neither a man nor a senior consultant, and I did not know this woman. Nevertheless, the midwife confirmed that the entire dynamic of the delivery changed from the moment I entered the room. The mother gave me

the reason: "You astounded me! You hadn't followed anything of the whole business and you arrive at an awkward
moment to take care of a baby who has not even come out!"
I take her words for a literal interpretation of what happened.
Indeed, if my arrival and the little I said triggered something,
it was the possibility for her to give birth to herself as well. I
was outside the matter, and I allowed her to give birth next
to me, so to speak; that is, to extract herself from the inner
circle that joined her to her child. In so doing, "seen from
the outside," her child could appear to her like a being different from her, and, as a result, she could let him poke his nose
outside.

In this we see that it is not enough to watch the monitoring devices to predict the imminence of delivery; one must
also consider boundaries and reference points, and mark the
function of each one. It is up to the baby to enter life; it is up
to the mother to exit pregnancy.

The Psychoanalytic Protocol

In the maternity ward as in the outside world, not everyone
should resort to psychoanalysis. It is not that psychoanalysts
are unable to confront the suffering related by their contem-
poraries, but that they can respond only to those who ask. An
arbitrary rule, some might say? In effect, an arbitrary rule,
but salutary and well thought out. A therapist always has the
right, if she has the physical strength, to take herself for a
"mental health emergency service" and to rush to the aid of
everyone in the room. It is to be feared, however, that playing the good Samaritan when families ask for nothing will
produce the reverse effect. In fact, locating the site of uncon-

scious desire that governs a subject can be done only as a function of the request and its effects; such are the rudiments of the psychoanalyst's work.

For myself, I sometimes read a newborn's medical file, as I would in my capacity as a psychiatrist or a psychologist. Nevertheless, I avoid it as much as possible. This is not a lack of professional conscientiousness; I simply do not want the "free-floating" way I listen to a patient to be governed in advance by a medical file. In 99 percent of cases, the elements that appear in the file can be found in the account the nursing staff has given me. There is a great difference between hearing something said and reading it in a file, since the former is already charged with all the affects the patient's request produced in the nurse.

The case of newborns is rather special. They are under guardianship, and their request depends on their parents' acknowledgment of it. If the parents refuse to share their children's suffering, I have no business intervening. That request may recur, in another place and time, and will then find a way to be heard. We must not close the door to that eventuality by imposing ourselves immediately after birth.

To those who find that argument "cruel," I will attempt to reply as I do to members of the staff who are frustrated that I do not intervene when they find a case alarming but when the parents ask for nothing: One must accept the fact that one cannot always change something in the life of people or their tragedies. To interfere without their consent would be worse than indifference. It would be a lack of respect, irresponsible and destined to failure, since it consists of refusing from the outset to take into consideration what motivates the suffering of subjects: unconscious desire. The list of those who "are doing this for your own good," "who wish you well," is too disreputable for a psychoanalyst to agree to add her name to it. That is one of the peculiarities of her practice.

In short, it is the parents' request, conveyed by members of the staff, that will put me in the position of a psychoanalyst. Since my job is to make room for the suffering word, I must be accountable only to it, whatever the real or imaginary needs of the hospital ward.

There must therefore be a boundary line to these interventions. That boundary is similar to the line drawn between the two rooms of the daycare center developed by Françoise Dolto, a line children were forbidden to cross on a bike or scooter. The line of separation in question was designed to protect the littlest ones from noise and spills. But, after all, why was it drawn one place rather than another? No one could remember. The regulation was as idiotic as it was inexorable, as Dolto herself admitted. In its very arbitrariness, that boundary nevertheless had a humanizing function of the utmost importance for these children. First, in articulating the rule for them and allowing them to argue about it, it allowed them to understand it. A truism? Not solely. If a child does not even grasp that, when he gets on a tricycle, he's the one driving, he is astounded when told he crossed the line because his feet pushed him beyond it. His understanding will be a revelation. This is illustrated in Dolto's talk with a toddler, excerpted from a private video recording:

> "That line is because, on the other side, babies are on the floor crawling. . . . If your daddy comes in with his motorcycle or car, he won't be allowed to go into the other room either."

"Oh yes he would, if Daddy comes, he'll come with his car and he'll go in there."

"Oh, do you think so? I don't. All you have to do is ask him tonight."

The next day:

"So, did you talk to him?"

"He said he won't come by car. But Mommy said that at home I can go into the living room on my tricycle."

"At home it's not the same thing. This is the Maison Verte, and here, it's not allowed. It applies to you, but it also applies to me, to your mommy, and to all the people who come here."

"—."

In this case, the child's humanization is also the pleasure of playing with the rule, of pretending to break it, and of bursting out laughing when he sees someone else has understood, of turning back because, finally, what counts most for him is the Maison Verte and he likes to stay there. In short, provided he is helped in that game, provided someone pays attention to his person, the pleasure of transgression is transformed into complicity.

It is in the same spirit that I began by establishing a boundary for my work at Béclère. Indeed, says psychoanalyst Denis Vasse, "with the boundary one does not repress, one does not protect oneself, one does not frighten. With the boundary, one speaks."[1] That is the aim of the request protocol I have established as a general rule. It is done so that we may speak and not only treat. To treat, in my position, would be to judge myself responsible for the behavior of these mothers and babies, and to present them with my good advice or my prescriptions, regardless of the story they might tell. That may be useful in an emergency, but there is often something better to be done.

KHADER AND THE EVIL EYE

A racket on the second floor of the maternity ward: A man's voice booms, shouts, rages. That is uncommon here. The voice is loud and sonorous, the whole floor is in on it. The husband of the patient in room thirty-two has been there for half an hour, and is making everyone anxious. He calls his wife every name in the book; the baby is terrified, he is screaming and crying his eyes out, which is hardly common at four days old. What is more, the father leaves the room and takes to task everyone passing by: midwives, nurses, doctors, new mothers. An orderly has to be called in before things settle down. Everyone calms the father as much as possible, reassures the baby with kindness, comforts the mother. Life resumes its tranquil pace on the floor, but room thirty-two is shaken. The next day, one of the midwives tells me about the previous day's commotion and recommends I see the baby, whom, she says, it would do some good; the mother agrees. I therefore go to room thirty-two.

"Hello, my name is Myriam Szejer, I was told you asked to see me about your son. What's going on?"

"You see, he cries all the time. He's sick. He had jaundice, and since this morning he's had conjunctivitis. With me it's different, I'm crying because I'm tired."

"What's your son's name?"

"His name is Khader. Well, no, his name is Azzedine, but my husband's parents think it's better for a good Muslim to be called Khader."

"They're religious?"

"Yes, especially my mother-in-law. They pay a lot of attention to those details, they don't fool around with tradition. That's how it is in my country, it's the husband's family that decides; and, with them, you aren't allowed to do anything wrong. But I prefer the name Azzedine."

"Has it always been that way with them?"

"Yes, and in any case they don't like me or my family. They say my brother and father are hopeless cases, that I won't know how to raise my children like a good Muslim."

"What about your husband?"

"I love him. But, since he's unemployed, his father says he's a good-for-nothing too and that he has to listen to him and do what he says. But it's not true. My father-in-law is traditional. As for my mother-in-law, she's very possessive; my husband is her only son, so you can imagine. . . . In the end, I got sick of it, and left my in-laws' house. My husband agreed. Now I'm afraid they'll kidnap Khader and bring him up in the tradition of their country. But my husband and I don't want that, we want to keep him with us."

Khader seemed to be sleeping. I addressed him, spoke to him about his names and the familial and cultural, if not political, stakes he represented. Khader became agitated. I then talked to him about the scene the day before: "You got agitated and you were very frightened yesterday, I think, when your father shouted . . ."

"No, no, my son wasn't afraid, even if my husband shouted a little loudly. A baby doesn't get afraid."

At these words, Khader had a violent spasm and stiffened his arms and legs. In the end, he relaxed and fell back to sleep. I took note of the simultaneity of the two phenomena and continued with the mother: "What happened yesterday?"

"Well, so my husband came, but he brought two friends with him. But he knows that during the first month you can't show a newborn to strangers, otherwise he attracts the evil eye. Where we come from, babies are veiled with a sheet when they go out, otherwise you know you're running the risk of bringing bad luck down on them. So I got mad, I told my husband he should've warned me and that I would have hidden the child in front of his friends. He got mad in turn, then things went from bad to worse."

I immediately thought of the conjunctivitis, which affected Khader only in the right eye, and I then addressed him: "Khader, you don't need to carry the evil eye in your body. You were born in France, as your parents wished. And here, to visit a newborn is to do him an honor, it doesn't bring bad luck on him. Your father and mother are respectful of the family's traditions, but they find it natural to practice the same customs as everyone here. Like your parents, you can bow to the same rules without feeling obliged to get sick."

"You're right, but there's something else: Khader sleeps all the time and never asks to eat. I don't understand why."

Khader did not let his mother finish her sentence. He began to move at that precise moment, woke up, and began to nurse at his mother's breast.

"You see, he still knows how to ask for what he needs."

"So much the better if I made a mistake."

"In any case, he understood you!"

I concluded our conversation at that moment and left, somewhat perplexed by that business of a weeping eye and an evil eye. Was it a belief, a superstition, or a tradition? Was I right to connect the symptom of Khader's conjunctivitis to the evil eye that frightened his mother? Should I have shared it with the child, in front of his mother, who saw her husband only as a link in the chain of a persecuting family? After all, I do not share their traditions; who was I to get mixed up in that matter? I left Béclère half reassured that day, a bit haunted by my own memories of those children's games where you cast spells "for fun."

Fortunately for everyone, the pediatrician, who came from the same country as the parents, was able to discuss the matter with the mother at length. She was well acquainted with the cultural environment of Khader's parents, and the conversation, it seems, was very warm. When I returned to the ward two days later, I went back to see Khader. I had been made to understand that he was doing better and that his mother's attitude had changed.

"It's great, Doctor, Khader doesn't have any more problems with his eyes. He's not crying anymore, he's got dry eyes, and he's not screaming anymore. It's incredible!"

The mother cuddled Khader and spoke into his ear for a few minutes.

"I saw the pediatrician, she says everything's back to normal. We talked a little, she's very nice."

"Did she reassure you?"

"Yes, she told me how it was for her when she had her first child in France, how difficult it was to explain to the family that her husband was caring for him."

"A little like for you, in fact?"

"Yes, but it's going to work out. My husband is putting together a changing table for Khader, he made a drawing for me, he even explained how he had to pay attention setting it up so that . . . so that I don't know what, I didn't understand a thing, but it was funny. His parents, well, they're his parents. But he's really helping me. When I get home, I'm going to tidy everything up because I know him; it won't be spick-and-span in the house. While I'm doing that, he'll take care of Khader. And afterward, we'll celebrate."

Everything was more or less returning to normal. Khader was not crying anymore, and he was eating. His mother was no longer worried and was making a new place for her husband; she had found someone qualified to speak with her about her country and the difficulties of expatriation; she felt ready to protect her child as she had known how to protect herself until then. The father was making himself busy. And I was forgetting my childish fears about the game of casting spells. In short, the word was put back into circulation, the same word that had erupted from the father's throat, and which veiled itself in the son's eye. Putting the word back into circulation allowed the roles to be reassigned: "You're the father, and you're not just the representative and victim of your family"; "You're the mother, and it's up to you to protect your child"; "You're your parents' son, and your parents' fears must not prevent you from seeing things clearly!"

THE REQUEST

For such words to come about, a protocol is needed that allows them to be really heard, and not simply noisily hurled about in the hallways or noted down in a medical file. It requires a quality of listening that makes it possible for members of the staff to do their screening, combined with the framework of a psychoanalytic session, which allows for listening and interpretation; in addition, it requires a consideration of the context, cultural in this case. The clear-sightedness of the midwives, the skill of the neonatal nurses, the talent of the pediatrician, the interpretation of the psychoanalyst: None of that in itself suffices as a guarantee. It is from collaboration that real care can emerge. For that collaboration to be regulated, once again, the roles have to be clarified. The protocol is like a monitor or a script consulted on a television set, so that everyone knows where he is. It is more than a prompter, then—one does not whisper a line to a suffering person, since she is the only one with a memory of it—it is a record, a guide that recalls who is who and at what point in the action the actors have arrived. I said I had to fight to get that protocol accepted. That is altogether logical. My idea was to transpose my office practice as a psychoanalyst to the hospital, inspired by the work conceived by Dolto with the Antony nursery. This was a new thing at Béclère, and no one had any reason to understand a priori the need for that protocol. I had to explain it. The preliminary meetings with every category of staff member were the opportunity for me to do so.

Through our discussions, we built something, since everything was unprecedented. Until then, like all psychoanalysts, I dealt with requests in my office or at the medical-psychological center, from people in a position to make them, and who made the effort to dedicate a part of their budget toward their treatment. Whether these requests were accepted, whether or not the people had the opportunity to discover the unconscious desire they were masking, that's another story. But they were responsible for the request they made to me. At the medical-psychological center and in my office, I also received children who had been placed in foster families, whom Children's Services sent to me. It is clear that the responsibility, or better, the guardianship in question, fell in that case to the institutions, and not to the person making the request. But, at the hospital, we were no longer dealing with a private psychoanalytic treatment or a consultation at the medical-psychological center, but with a psychoanalytic consultation within the institution. In constructing a frame-work in which speech could be understood analytically, I was now dealing with a twofold problem. On the one hand, who was making the request in the maternity ward? And who in the ward could serve as mediator to these requesting subjects, as Children's Services served as an intermediary to children placed in foster care?

Which request should I hear, or, if one prefers, whom should I go to see? The baby, or the mother and father? I would say all three, or at least the mother and the child if the father is not there. I cannot address one without speaking to the other; I cannot hear one without listening to the other. My response is not as cryptic as some might believe: I simply mean that things are very intimately intertwined in that peri-natal and postdelivery space.

The place of the symptom is tripartite, as we saw with the story of Khader. The father shouts, that is the warning signal; the little boy has conjunctivitis, that is the symptom strictly speaking; the mother is in the midst of a familial and cultural conflict, that is the crux of the problem. The place of the symptom may be the child, the mother, the father, or all three at once. When the particulars are given me, everything takes place in private with these three. I spoke to Khader directly and that had the effect of making his symptom disappear, but it also changed the mother's position in relation to her husband and child. For Karina, the baby who wouldn't eat, I first spoke to the mother, allowing her to identify with her own mother and to become a mother in turn, to break down the prohibition. Was it the effect of these words on the mother that allowed the child to drink, or was it the words addressed to the child and heard by the mother? Probably both. There is, however, an exception to the protocol in the case of a birth where the child will be placed for adoption. There, only the words spoken to the child count, even though these words are those of the mother. Either she says them directly to the child, or, declining to see him, asks me to transmit them to him. I believe that the symptom functions within the father-mother-child triad. It sometimes affects the integrity of the child's body, but the trigger can also be a mother's tears, or a father who breaks his leg or becomes hysterical. I am often called the "psychoanalyst for babies," and that is how I am sometimes introduced to the mothers. But, as I have been intent to show, I work with the affective and sensorial continuum in newborns. That said, professionals give me many labels when they indicate my existence to the mothers. These names are more or less warranted, depending on whether they come from new recruits or from staff members who know me well. I am sometimes "the psychiatrist," sometimes "the psychologist," or "someone named Myriam who could help you," or "the child shrink." They have a certain resistance to speaking quite simply of the "psychoanalyst" because, in their minds, that would connote long-term treatment and patent insanity ("all the same, we're not going to tell them that they or their baby are crazy!"). And yet, mothers remain in the maternity ward for a week at most, and I only go by Béclère twice a week. At most one, two, or three sessions can be held. I do not say that the mother and child will always come out of our conversations with a light heart, but one to three sessions are often enough for everyone to get out of something that from the time of the birth was jeopardizing their future. And everyone who wishes is free to enter psychoanalysis subsequently if seriously disabling structural problems reveal themselves at a later time. At that moment, I point parents who ask me toward practitioners I trust. The important thing is that their request be reformulated in another context, outside the maternity ward.

THE STAFF, MEDIATORS OF THE WORD

Who can fulfill that function of mediation between the requester and the psychoanalyst, as guardian institutions do within the framework of a consultation with a child? Midwives, nurses, pediatricians, social workers, obstetricians, or gynecologists: In other words, all who are in continuous contact with babies. It is they who "point out," who sniff out, who take the pulse of the roomfuls of patients to know whether "things are all right" or if the parents must be told that I can help their baby in distress. It is they who transmit the wishes of these parents to me. It is they, in short, who are the guardians of the protocol.

Unlike the guardians of the gates of the law in Kafka's *The Trial,* they are there to facilitate access to the word. If they call on me, saying that Mrs. So-and-So has agreed to see me, I go see Mrs. So-and-So. If, rarely, they tell me that, in their view, the lady in room eight may be in need of my services but that she refuses to see me, I do not go. Similarly, when someone from the outside points out a baby or a mother to me, but no member of the staff thought it advisable to do so, I act only after having the mother asked if she wishes to meet me. We are connected, the staff and I, and there is no interference from higher-ups in that exchange between us. The staff members know it and, in that exchange, necessity dictates the law; the trust we show in each other is the condition for our collaboration.

Of course, that mainspring of my work did not function from the first day as if it were natural. I had to sensitize people to what I wanted to do. My discourse was new to them, sometimes upsetting, because some imagined they would have to "play the shrink" in addition to attending to their daily workload. But their delicacy amazed me. I was afraid at first that they would send me to mothers who did not really need me, or that they would do it against their will, or, even worse, that they would not refer anyone to me. Also, I initially set up two stages to the referral. They spoke to me about the babies they thought I ought to see, and I arbitrated to say if it was within my area of competence or not; only then did they suggest to the mothers that I might come. Very quickly, we began to skip a stage, since they gauged the need very skillfully. They were able to identify what was of concern to me so well that they could be authorized to ask people directly if they wanted to see me. I arrive in the morning, I am told that Mr. or Mrs. So-and-So is waiting for me, and I go. Under unusual circumstances, it may happen that I am referred to someone when there is clearly no reason for it; my principle in that case is to go, to respect the request of the mothers who asked to see me. There is also a problem of staff rotation: I must periodically explain again the meaning of the work. Personal discussions, hallway conversations with "old-timers," or a few memos generally suffice to integrate the "newcomers" into our team.

In general, midwives prefer to work in the delivery room rather than in postdelivery, because of the emotion it produces, the sense of responsibility, if not the "entertaining" side it entails. The joy of bringing a child into the world has no equivalent, in fact, and the wealth of emotions it elicits is never exhausted. Nevertheless, many of the midwives who have made this protocol work have attested that they found a different enjoyment in this new work in postdelivery. There is something human about their interventions that makes their work lighter and more interesting. My well-being and that of the newborns depend on the humanity and efficiency they demonstrate. In that sense, they are true *living probes* working with patients, to use psychoanalyst Lucien Kokh's expression.

Understanding of the Context

The staff members' mediating function engages everyone's talents and sensitivity. It works only through their understanding of the context. Indeed, sorting out what is abnormal suffering and what is a passing case of the blues, attributable to fatigue, takes more than a nose for such things. One must understand, as they do, that the distress of the baby blues has a structuring role, because it allows the mother-child relation to be set in place, and that therefore one must respect it and listen to it if it asks for that. They know how to distinguish a harmless case of baby blues from situations where something isn't running smoothly, for the newborn or the parents.

They also know, as I have already said, that there are cases when I will not intervene on any pretext, for example, when the mother refuses my intervention. What does it mean that she refuses? Certainly not that someone has inadequately explained the meaning of my intervention, since staff members are very clear on that point. Parents always have good reasons for refusing to accept a recommendation that they meet with me. Either it is simply not the right time, or, unconsciously, they want the child to remain in the place of the symptom. It is then up to the pediatrician to intervene to comfort the child; it is up to me to comfort the staff and to make them understand that their request is not necessarily the patient's.

All of that requires a great deal of perseverance and tenacity on everyone's part, given the resistance that can be provoked. It may happen, for example, that a doctor from a nearby ward, if he is not properly informed about these practices, will say he is dismayed: He asks me to go see a new mother, and I refuse because the patient did not wish it. You can imagine the misunderstandings. In addition, in a case like that, it is better not to see the patient in question; otherwise, she may be made to suffer because of territorial and power conflicts that do not regard her. The most pleasant form of resistance, because it is the most intelligent, is that which permits itself to be overcome by humor. For example, there was an obstetrician who ran into me one day on the ward and asked me to see a fifty-year-old patient of his. He remained evasive about the reasons for that request, explaining that the woman had become pregnant via in vitro fertilization in England and had returned to France to give birth.

Everything had gone marvelously well; she was radiant, beaming, and the baby was doing well. This occurred at a time when Italian fertility specialist Severino Antinori was first attracting media coverage—"What, that scandalous doctor who gives babies to grandmothers!"—and that sort of birth was considered heresy. My colleague was thus asking himself a great number of questions about these mothers of a new kind, and undoubtedly set out to shed light on them by asking me to see his patient "in an iconographic capacity." That colleague is unanimously revered at the Antoine Béclère Hospital for his competence and his interest in research, and I also respect him highly. Nevertheless, I politely refused to see his patient, arguing that, from what I had been able to learn from the staff in the meantime, her condition appeared excellent, and she clearly did not need anything. Since I was also familiar with this man's wit, I wondered out loud whether he was not the real petitioner. I added that, if that were the case, I was by all means entirely at his disposal. He laughed good-heartedly.

An understanding of the context also includes the sociocultural context in which each of the intervening parties is steeped. And here, there is no pseudopsychoanalytic neutrality at stake. Each has her own area of competence and specificity of course, but it is important not to mask the type of social connection in which we are each inscribed, if we are to claim to help inscribe children in a new social connection. Discussions among ourselves are always informal. I do not call meetings; I prefer the corridors since, as at conventions, it is there that the most important things always get said. Personal views are never rejected in the name of so-called professional discretion, nor are requests regarding a personal problem.

Common sense and friendly relations are the minimal condition that allows for a collaboration that can serve newborns. I can affirm that, in Khader's case, it was the collaboration between the pediatrician and the psychoanalyst that made it possible to reestablish everyone's place in that family.

Within the framework of the maternity ward, psychoanalysis operates through the protocol. The first notable effect, which surprised everyone on the ward, beginning with myself, was, as I said, the impressive quantity of material that came to the surface after childbirth. None of the women who worked there had suspected the avalanche of confidences they would receive when they took the time to listen. Every time they sat down in a room for five minutes, they could not get away again. Some gradually realized that the material was an assault as much as an object of fascination. They dreaded it, but did not feel they had the strength to put a stop to it. They were soon comforted by the idea that they could hand the patient off to me when they reached the limit of their availability and competence. A number of them saw only benefits in the fact that these suffering mothers were not just left there with their words and no response, and that they could address them to me: From initial curiosity, they moved on to cooperation.

It may now be clearer why I wish to bear witness in this book. I want it to be a memoir of what was built with the Béclère staff, what made it possible to practice psychoanalysis in the maternity ward. The combination of their expertise and understanding of the context on the one hand, and my understanding of scientific studies and of the ethical requirements of psychoanalysis on the other, made possible an unprecedented experiment with newborns. The exchanges, even the "swapping of expertise" among us (as one speaks of swapping technology) sustained the vitality of that experiment. These exchanges cannot be the object of a univocal theory: It would be pure fiction to claim so. It is human connections that determine for each person the *time for understanding,* and, on a daily basis, allow for the practice of psychoanalysis through the protocol. I have no truth to proffer regarding such connections, only a tribute to pay them. They naturally brought me my own *moment to conclude.* When and why can interpretation come into being, what is its urgency, and what are its effects: on the baby blues, on prevention, in the case of babies placed for adoption? When and why can one say that a baby is a subject? What does that practice with babies offer for the psychoanalysis of adults? These are the questions we now need to address.

5. *From Birth to Life's Limbo: A Closer Look at the Baby Blues*

"Everyone who has known me, everyone without exception, believes I am dead. My own conviction that I exist is unanimously opposed. . . . That alone suffices—not, of course, to kill me—but to push me back within the confines of life, in a place suspended between heaven and hell, in limbo, in short." —MICHEL TOURNIER

The three- or four-day period following birth is an uncertain time, because it is then that the birth to symbolic life must be decided. Let us call it the period of limbo, to signify the threshold at the edge of life that holds the child. It is, as we shall see, the moment of a choice for the newborn and for her parents. The child must choose to make room for her unconscious desire; her parents must acknowledge this desiring and unique child. If, for some reason, the parents are not with the child after birth, someone must show the child how to recognize her history as her own, so that she can come to terms with her desire. That critical moment of limbo is revealed in all its clinical clarity through the baby blues and through confidential childbirth (when a child is given up at birth). Although the first is as common as the second is rare, both raise the crucial question of the connection and communication between the new being and those who engendered her. That question contains in germ the entire problem of the human being's acceptance of life.

Born to Life

The child is born, the child is there. Two or three days have gone by since his birth. The mother slowly recovers from her emotions and fatigue. The father calms down as well. Any scars (episiotomy, cesarean) still smart a little, but the baby's presence helps make them bearable. The baby is a wonder, the mother never gets tired of looking at him, even when she is groggy. He's lost a little weight, but the doctors say that's normal.

And then, at the slightest thing, without knowing why, the mother can't take it anymore. Or rather, she changes moods moment by moment. She's cheerful for an hour and then, suddenly, nothing's going right anymore. She felt pain when her milk came in, and immediately thought, "I won't make it." The baby is bothered by a digestive problem or is spitting up, and she sees that as a sign that she's incapable of taking care of him. She tells herself, "I have everything I need to be happy," and that thought alone makes her desperately sad. Then she cries. Not a little tear: a torrent! The baby, sensitive to his mother's annoyance, begins to echo it. The mother, finding confirmation for the idea that she really is doing everything to ensure that things don't work out for him, feels worse. In short, she's got the blues, and she sings it solo and in a duet.

The staff is quite familiar with baby blues. At the morning staff meeting, one regularly hears lines like: "I've got nine crying, but apart from that there's nothing serious." Or someone comes to tell me: "Mrs. Dos Santos is crying too much"; "Mrs. Durieux is crying in a very peculiar way"; "Mrs. Taulay's behavior with her child suggests to me that things aren't going very well, she isn't really responding to the baby's demands"; and so on.

A COMMON AILMENT

Nothing about all that is really alarming. Let me explain myself: It is valid from a physiological point of view, and no doubt even desirable. The "standard" case of baby blues is very common, affecting 70 to 90 percent of new mothers, according to different estimates. In addition, it always appears on about the third or fourth day.

Why at that time? Probably because the baby blues correspond to a rhythm, a natural human cycle. For the baby, it is the moment when the type of communication she has with her mother changes. Her cries, which until then seemed to be an immediate reaction to her internal perceptions, become the first suggestions of a dialogue, as demonstrated by Cyrulnik's observations, which I related in chapter 3. The baby is already addressing, if not a constituted other, at least entities different from herself, and different from one another. For her part, the mother has had the time to observe that the child is not really a part of herself. If she still expressed that hope through her terms of endearment—"my little one," "my baby"—the care given the baby, and the words of family and friends directed exclusively to her, can give the mother the impression that she is being somewhat cast aside. It is thus dawning on her that she and her child make two! That truth, which she of course knows intellectually, depresses her because she is now experiencing it in her body, in her perceptions, and in her thoughts. In fact, the transformation of her body, particularly when her milk comes in—which also occurs on about the third day—comes about in relation to her child. That too is the beginning of an exchange.

This common case of baby blues resolves itself on its own, and the staff interferes little, except to facilitate intimate contact between the mother and her child. Nevertheless, the baby blues must not be confused with more marked depressions.

Psychiatrically speaking, postpartum depression in the strict sense appears later. It usually occurs after the mother has gone home, whereas, oddly, everything was going well in the maternity ward. A classic case of baby blues can also drag on interminably, hence becoming more serious. There is also the case of so-called puerperal psychosis, a serious melancholic condition with overtones of delirium, which may occur independent of any apparent baby blues, or, on the contrary, may look like a disturbing aggravation of the baby blues. It is usually observed among subjects already known for their fragility, but it can arise with a first birth, or may even constitute something like a relapse during a second. Fortunately, its frequency is dropping thanks to earlier pharmacological and psychological treatment.

Melancholic depression, puerperal psychosis, and withdrawal psychosis are extreme cases that may be related to a crisis experienced by the mother. Her history and her past suffering are at issue at that point, much more than the presence of the new arrival. Nevertheless, they can place the child in danger; he himself may become psychotic. As Dolto has said, such an imbalance on the mother's part is, for the new-born, "an eerie appeal that provokes him to give his own life back [to his mother] in order to later feel justified in letting go of her and leaving. [It is] a vicious circle from which psychotics cannot escape because, to escape it, they must first pump new life into their mother. Once that is done, they are fastened onto her, fused with her, not knowing any longer how to separate from her. . . . If someone could explain to newborns what was happening to them and to their parents, they would not experience any depression."[1] The psychoanalyst may intervene to see that this story is explained at a minimal level to the mother and child, and may begin to undo that pathogenic connection.

Is there no mother who does not get the baby blues? There are such mothers, no doubt, but that's because they anticipated them and warded them off during pregnancy.

Anthropologists tell us that, in many African societies, mothers do not experience that phenomenon. In these societies, where there is a highly symbolic ritual to welcome the birth and the responsibility of motherhood, baby blues supposedly do not exist. Let us note that these are societies, on the one hand, that take the incest taboo very seriously and concretely, and, on the other, where socialization is marked by very rigorous initiation rites, particularly for men. The notion of a kinship tie is thus transmitted in a very different way than it is in France or the United States, and the social framework plays a stabilizing role it no longer has in many Western countries.

Hence, particular importance is given to brothers, sisters, and members of the clan in general in the rearing of a younger child. This is less frequent in my country. The child's means of identification in such countries is entirely different from the individualist battlefield where we sometimes wallow. When the ideology of "every man for himself" is imposed on "unwed mothers," as they used to be called disdainfully, they find themselves alone against all, and the only anchors their children have are the employees at children's aid societies.

Similarly, it is common in sub-Saharan Africa for a woman to carry her child until he reaches the age of two years; if circumstances do not allow it, another woman from the maternal clan will step in. The child is carried constantly, spoken to continuously, and inevitably less of a victim to the "holes of words" that so greatly affect the earliest years. By contrast, in a contemporary Western family, one sees many fewer women, relatives or in-laws, helping new mothers. The interdependence of the past seems to play a lesser role. Mothers then "turn back" to their partners who, no doubt, are no better than men were in the past at knowing how to face a new mother's problems.

Men, who are of course much more present in the first moments, are, in the end, welcomed to the maternity wards only as the mothers' husbands or partners, not as fathers. In the hospital, everything is done for the mothers, their bellies, their scars, their breasts, and anyone approaching the newborn is tolerated only as a function of the mothers. Fatherhood will truly come into being only with the homecoming, when the mother will ask the father to get close to the baby, to change her, etc. It is the mother and the baby who will make him a father.

There is no denying that one woman or another may be spared the baby blues, thanks to particularly strong support from those around her. It is nevertheless true that these common baby blues arise at a fundamental moment for the three partners—father, mother, and child—and raise an essential question for them about what filiation is. Sometimes these blues exceed the normal intensity. That is, one of the three shows that he or she is suffering too much, and cannot come out of it on her or his own. It may be the mother or the child, but it may also be the father, since the father can also get the baby blues. It is in these cases that, through the protocol, I ask pediatricians, midwives, and nurses to propose that the partners meet with me. If our schedules do not coincide, they can still arrange for an appointment at my office.

The Baby Sets the Tone

Are we to understand the baby blues as attributable to the baby or as set in motion by him? In other words, is it the mother's depression or the baby's? The depression stems from both of them, but it is the newborn who triggers the baby blues in his mother. Just as the mother's milk comes in as a response to the child's cries, or at least his presence, the baby blues are provoked by the child.

Let us imagine a case where the mother does not have her child near her. Does that absence spare her from the baby blues? Consider women whose children have been transferred at birth to the intensive care unit. These women do not get the baby blues on the fourth day. They are certainly worried and depressed, sad at the very least, because of that immediate separation. They are depressed at having to give up what they had imagined were the first connections to their child, connections that could not take place after the birth.

This is a reactive depression in the true sense of the term, a depression in reaction to a difficult situation that has been imposed on them. But it is not the same depression as the baby blues, and does not have the same tone or "flavor." These women do not say, as those with the baby blues do: "I'm crying and I don't know why. I have everything I need to be happy, but I am incapable of taking care of my child." They say it is painful to be separated from their own flesh and blood, and to be unable to do anything to aid their babies when they suffer, because circumstances do not allow it. In a pinch, they may reproach themselves for being unable to do something, namely, to produce a healthy child, which a woman with the baby blues will not do, except in unusual cases. Women whose children have gone to the neonatal unit at birth get the baby blues, but later. They wait until they are reunited with their baby. Usually, these women begin to cry, and not just for joy, when the child returns to their side. The presence of the child awakens in them the need to celebrate that reunion with a full-blown case of baby blues. The baby as well will not fail to chime in, since, let us recall, a baby immediately separated from her mother at birth cries in much greater quantity than one placed on her mother's belly. When the child is placed on the mother's belly, she gets to know the outside world with the mother, which is entirely different from being separated for a few instants to be given routine care. In the former case, she has fewer reasons to cry.

In the same way, there are well-known cases of adoptive mothers who, three or four days after the adopted child arrives home, begin to cry and to voice the well-known complaint: "I don't know what's wrong. It's idiotic, I'm crying even though we waited so long for this child and wanted him so much, but I can't help myself. Don't tell me he's cute, I know that and it makes me cry even more."

The baby blues are not only a matter of hormones, as some pretend to believe. The condition is certainly reinforced by fatigue and a hormonal imbalance, but it is nonetheless not a medical symptom.

The baby blues are about a little being of flesh and blood, medically incomplete and dependent, reputed to be immature in many respects, who nevertheless decides that it's his turn to play. It is up to him to trigger, by his presence, a process of exchange with the only woman he knows well. He is, if not the cause of the baby blues, then at least the condition for that depression. Without him beside the mother, there would be no depression. That depression must be understood as the mother's act of taking in her child's active need for communication. In doing so, and in return, she appeals to him specifically in his place as a human *other* whom she attempts to recognize, if only, in this instance, with a few cries and the gnashing of teeth. The moment of the baby blues is one of the first steps toward this specifically human dimension. The way the child responds to the mother's depression will mark the beginning of active communication. Up to then, as I said, he was crying to express, without mediation, his bodily discomfort. A droning without commentary, like reading the pages of a phone book. That is how it used to be understood in maternity wards. The cries served as a warning signal, an automatic and simultaneous translator of the baby's health; to verify that an infant was doing well at birth, someone lightly slapped his bottom to make him cry. We have evolved since then. With the baby blues, the droning becomes intentional and plays a tune, as it were; it becomes the language modulations I mentioned earlier. If that attempt at communication fails, the child's entire body will become the place of language through its symptoms.

That attempt at communication turns, for example, on lactation, that is, on the oral drives to satisfy alimentary needs. Of lactation and the baby blues, it has been said: when the morale drops, the milk rises. Remember the lady in black discussed in chapter 3? That woman was referred to me because of the inconsolable sadness that had overtaken her, but the call might very well have come from her daughter, Eva, who was crying in pain. Her mother attributed her guilt to her failure to produce milk—"I'm not even capable of feeding my baby." What was needed was rather to give voice to what was being played out in the mourning, the birth, and the absence of milk. The words spoken were able to induce the milk to come in and to put an end to tears, because they set right an "off-kilter" communication established between Eva and the lady in black. The lady in black, finally able to make room for the child as other—a child who until then had been masked by the omnipresent memory of the dead—again discovered she was a nurturing mother, and Eva was welcomed.

The Tripartite Place of the Symptom

It often happens that the newborn designates the father or mother as the one who must be spoken to. That is a very clear sign of the fact that the newborn is active in triggering the baby blues. It is somewhat equivalent to what one encounters in older children in cases of symbolic payment.* In my office, I once saw a child under two who had his payment in hand, but who refused to come into the room. I of course agreed not to hold his session, as he was instructing me in a roundabout way, and therefore spoke to his mother to tell her so. I had hardly started to speak when she began to cry and to give a long account of her own troubles. The child, in some sense, refused me the symbolic payment so that I would listen to his mother and not to him. Once that "obstacle" was overcome, the work with him resumed in the following sessions.

The child can point out in the parent's discourse precisely "where it hurts." I was asked one day to see a new mother on the maternity ward whose pregnancy had been particularly difficult. This woman had fallen into a depressive state in the second month of pregnancy, and had contracted rubella in the sixth month, putting her child's health in danger. The reason for her breakdown in the second month was that she realized that the man with whom she conceived the child was not "for her"; he was "beneath contempt." She realized at that moment that, by living with him, she was giving up everything that makes a woman a woman. She confided that all her hopes of seduction, of sexual satisfaction, of complicity, had been disappointed. Furthermore, shortly thereafter, when she left to get some rest, her mother, the child's grand-

---

* Symbolic payment is the practice established by Françoise Dolto, whereby a child not yet old enough to support himself nevertheless pays for his session with a hazelnut or a stone, in short, with any object without particular significance that can take the place of money. In spite of his financial dependence, he thereby becomes able to express his desire to have a session or refuse by not paying.

mother, attempted suicide, an attempt that my patient immediately interpreted as the grandmother's fear that her daughter, upon having a child, would slip away from her grasp. In fact, the grandmother seemed all-powerful, demanding everything from her daughter, and considering her her "baby." The mother was saddened, and, even more, disabled, by the grandmother's action. She had to escape the authority of her own mother; she could no longer be her mother's "baby" if she wanted to be a mother to her own. The woman then spoke of her father: a "spineless good-for-nothing," incapable of procuring joy for anyone.

Every time she spoke of her father that way, her baby punctuated her words with a whimper. The child was reacting to the idea her mother had of the grandfather as if to indicate where the shoe pinched. The funny thing was that the child was right. She knew what was going on. Her mother, probably hearing her cries, was completely flabbergasted: "So what, then, I'm treating my husband like my father? The spineless one is my father, not my husband."

"You have to be able to make a place for the father you've chosen for your child."

"Yes, that's right, not the place of *my* father!"

In fact, the father was nothing like the grandfather, far from it. This "shiftless" person "beneath contempt" had, in point of fact, come across as the epitome of virility and authority to staff members at the hospital, where he had accompanied the mother during the ultrasounds. Preoccupied with everything, accepting nothing without complaint, even coming to an appointment in place of his wife, he seemed more like a conquering superman, according to the nursing staff. But, for that woman, the man she had chosen could only be similar in every respect to her father, despite all evidence to the contrary.

When I saw this woman a second time at her request, the weight of the repetition had become perceptible to her, and her condemnation was transformed into a complaint: "What can you do with a husband who doesn't take concrete responsibility for being a father?" That man, in fact, had no passion for diapers or baby bottles, and seemed uninterested in caring for the child. The distress manifested in her complaint contrasted with the open seductiveness of her apparel and in the delight she took in relating her recent professional success. Seeing her recovered and able to manage things, I advised her to compromise with her husband and to give him time to become a father. She had wanted that child, he really had not. She had to count on her daughter to make him a father, now or later. She herself was convinced that she needed to work on her own issues, and asked me for the address and phone number of a psychoanalyst. Perhaps a psychoanalyst will allow her to move beyond the statement she made about her husband at the end of our conversation: "He's a man from the old days, like my father."

The newborn, his mother, and his father can thus be successively at the center of the inquiry raised by the baby blues. The question then arises: If the place of the symptom is tripartite, to whom does one speak? For myself, I never speak to one without speaking to the other. If it is difficult for fathers to be present, I speak to the mother in front of the child, and to the child in front of the mother. In the case of Karina, who refused to nurse, I first addressed the mother and advised her to place her daughter directly against her skin. Karina's elder brother had died just before birth, and her parents, to ward off fate, had not wanted to make any plans for the arrival of their younger child. Let me add an element I have not yet mentioned regarding her. In speaking of the "forbidden" child, her mother mentioned a coincidence that Karina immediately remarked on by making noisy sucking motions: Karina was the younger daughter, just as her mother was the youngest of her brothers and sisters. The mother realized she had never spoken in front of her daughter about her own parents, who lived in Hungary and had not been able to come see Karina. As a result, our conversation consisted of quite simply relating family matters, making Karina a witness to the fact that she was not limited to her nuclear family, but came from a family line. She was no longer in the place of the forbidden child, but was placed once more along the chain of her ancestors. From there, the mother could more easily accede to the necessary identification first-time mothers have with their own mothers. It is identifying with one's own mother that allows one to become a mother in turn, and that identification was particularly difficult in her case because it was complicated by a long history of infertility. It was only then that I addressed Karina directly, to tell her that, unlike her elder brother, her capacity to live depended on her alone, on whether she decided to take nourishment.

It seemed necessary to me to speak both to the baby and to the mother. I maintain with Dolto that "children speak their parents and, conversely, they are in their parents." The symptom operates within the mother-child-father triad. It may affect the integrity of the child's body through the mother's tears, or through the father's irritation in the mother's hospital room. The child can also be singled out as one who does not eat, who does not wake up, who rejects. In every case where I intervene, I act in such a way that words can be placed over the contents of the unconscious, so that they can circulate among the three protagonists and allow speech to be pried open.

That need for a good word and for a circulation of speech begins with the proper form of address to be used with these three people. What are we to call them? In certain maternity wards, new mothers are called "mommy": the mommy "in 15," the mommy "of little Grégoire," "that mommy who cries so much." No one protests, because there's no ill intention. But a woman who has given birth is a woman before being a mother. As for being "mommy," the privilege to call her that is reserved for her children—unless, in calling her "mommy," the nursing staff are thinking of their own mothers. No one would say such things, no doubt, if fathers were allowed to have more of a presence in maternity wards. Alas, they are not granted a place worthy of their status. When fathers are permitted to sleep in the maternity ward, when they are given the right to come at any hour of the day and night, they may have, in everyone's eyes, a role other than that of taking the dirty laundry back home. They will have more time to give their partners the compliments they so like to give, to bring flowers that perfume mother and child as much as they enhance the father.

If the father is recognized as a man, not only by the mother but also by the hospital staff, he will then be able to reintroduce femininity to the woman who has just given birth and whose body has been more or less roughly treated. Let us give a harmless example. Ever since obstetrician Frederick LeBoyer introduced the idea, one of the tasks that has often fallen to men is to bathe the baby after birth. Unfortunately, we have reached the point of neglecting to ask the men their opinion. They are intimidated, and may be reluctant to touch the baby. Some undertake it, it must be said, in defiance of common sense. But has anyone simply explained to them that the aim of the operation is not to wash their baby but to link them to the body bath that began without them?

As for the way one introduces and names oneself, it is of the utmost importance. That is why, as pointless as it might seem, I never fail to introduce myself when I enter a room. This is not merely a question of courtesy. I say who I am and why I have come, to the parents and to the children.

Interpretation

For a psychoanalyst, speaking sometimes leads to interpretation. The interpretation can be addressed to the parents or to the child, depending on the situation; both (or all three) will hear it in any case. Let me insist on the newborn's presence, in the sense one speaks of an actor's presence. The child may react to a word that touches him through a movement of his head, a spasm, or a cry.

Granted. But what about when the child is sleeping? He is nonetheless present onstage. We must always be careful to speak of or to the sleeping child in the same manner as when he seems to be awake. We can make noise (in moderation) and speak around the baby without disturbing his sleep, but it will disturb him if, for example, we rouse him by leaning over his crib to speak to him. In other words, when we address him, he always responds "Present!" Without comparing the two situations more than we ought, we may in this regard consider Dolto's account of analytic sessions with a person in a coma.[2] Psychoanalysis is not rehabilitation, she says in substance, regarding that strange and overpowering case history, and we have the advantage of being able to work as psychoanalysts with people who are comatose. These people, in the passivity of their comas, are extremely receptive, though obviously not expressive. They have a dreamlike memory of the content of the session when they come out of the coma. That, she says, is because, beyond the physical person, "the subject of desire and the subject of one's own history are certainly present."

That seems valid to me for newborns as well. For a mother who undergoes a cesarean delivery under general anesthesia, I suggest to the staff that they speak to her to inform her of the child's arrival. I persist in ignoring the half-smiles that such a suggestion never fails to provoke, because I know that at least the young mother will feel less frustrated upon awakening, knowing that she was allowed to participate in that way. I have a friend, an orthopedic surgeon, now retired, who never neglected to speak to his unconscious patients during surgery because, he said, it helped them recuperate more quickly.

Above all, interpretation following childbirth remains preventive. I see children in profound crisis, and, on principle, do not see them again after the time they spend in the maternity ward. As I said, that period is four days at most for a normal delivery, seven in the case of a cesarean section. In so little time, the aim of the interpretation given the child of the contents of her mother's or father's unconscious, which are affecting her development, is to liberate her from the symptom. In parallel, the interpretation given the mother or father, about the questions the child raises for them, tends to allow them to find a harmony between their history and their parenthood. In some sense, it consists of dealing out a new hand of cards, which the birth has shuffled. Indeed, if they can begin a new hand upon leaving the maternity ward, there is nothing that says they cannot ask something more of the analyst. Thus it happened that a couple and their baby asked to see me while I was away from the hospital. They were given the address and phone number of my office, and they came to consult me there. Their request concerned their child, but it was the father who then undertook psychoanalysis with me.

Working with the newborn makes it possible to reexamine the problem of interpretation. More often than usual, one has to wonder with a newborn: What did I interpret, or how did the interpretation help him abandon his symptom? Of course, the psychoanalyst's expertise plays a role. It is up to her to allow the protagonists' words to explain the knots they are tied up in, in the Latin sense of *explain*, namely, to *undo, open out*. As a result, if there is interpretation, it may well be that of the analyst, but it may also be a mother's or father's word, which reveals itself when it is taken as a witness. When we say we interpret, let us pronounce it the old way: one *inter-prets,* lends between, speech *inter-prets* between the one who makes the appeal with his symptom, those to whom that symptom is addressed, and the psychoanalyst, who respects the imperative to see that the word circulates. I have had a few concrete testimonies of this from women I saw at intervals of several years, for several successive deliveries.

I saw Mrs. Ormani for a case of baby blues following the

birth of her first daughter, Elsa. The child was hospitalized in the kangaroo unit because of low birth weight, and she displayed no appetite, to her mother's great despair. The birth had been difficult because of hemorrhaging during the delivery. We know that Dolto believes such hemorrhaging puts the child in danger, as if one were "throwing out the baby with the bathwater." The pain of childbirth had revived the mother's memory of violent abdominal cramps, for which she had been hospitalized at age eight, at the same time and in the same hospital as her mother, who had been admitted following a miscarriage. It reminded her as well of the cesarean section she had undergone a year earlier to deliver her son, Alexandre, who died ten days after birth. The day of our meeting, Mrs. Ormani was able to tell her daughter about all that, with myself as witness. Elsa smiled at her words, and soon demanded to eat. Mrs. Ormani still remembered this three years later, when I saw her again for a new birth: "Elsa is perfectly healthy, you know. Every time there was a problem, I thought again of our conversation and of her smile. I did what we did at the time: I told her what was going on, and everything worked out. When I was hospitalized two and a half years ago, I explained to her that she was going to go to Italy to stay with her aunt because I wasn't feeling well. I told her why I wasn't feeling well, and that I would see her again when I was better. It went off without a hitch."

Elsa was feeling better, but Mrs. Ormani had not gotten out of her own difficulties. Therapy for her depression at the time of Elsa's birth made it possible, three years later, for her to give birth under good conditions, and in joy, to a son, Guillaume. One of the exciting things about psychoanalysis is that its progress affects both the patient and the analyst. Interpretations are shared (in this case, between Mrs. Ormani and me) and their effects can be both immediate (for Elsa) and delayed (for Mrs. Ormani and, indirectly, for Guillaume).

Psychoanalyst Alain Didier-Weill, to indicate what is at stake in psychoanalytic interpretation, uses a valuable musical metaphor, the expression "blue note," dear to jazz musicians. The blue note is the note the listener hopes to hear at the peak of listening pleasure, when it "pushes [him] to hear the appeal of a certain note that is not yet there, but whose tension, produced by the encounter between the harmony and the melodic notes already played, leads [him] to suppose it is not futile to expect it."[3] It is the silence following a piece by Mozart—which is still Mozart, according to the famous saying. It is not only the pleasure someone with a notion of the history of composition feels when, for example, he can finish a phrase "in the manner of" Verdi or Louis Armstrong. After all, that would be more difficult for Bach or Coltrane. It is rather the note hoped for and yet unexpected, which, when I hear it, "makes me cross a threshold that, without it, I would no doubt not have dared cross—a threshold to a world whose great novelty lies in the fact that, in it, the power of the unheard-of rules: the power to awaken me, by teaching me that everything sensible I may have heard up to then was, without my knowing it, under the ascendancy of the unheard-of." That hope, that "unheard-of," that expectation are what the newborn cries out to anyone willing to hear it; and I will not resist the parallel between the baby blues and the blue note. Psychoanalysis is effective, paradoxically, because it remains an art. Whether interpretation tends toward poetry, as Lacan hoped, or toward music, as Didier-Weill suggests, it, like the blue note, ought to be condensed into "a signifier stripped of all meaning, around which all the other notes articulate the subject I did not know I was."

IN AN UNCERTAIN LIMBO

The fetus's moral principle, said Dolto, is vampirism: in the first place, to live and to grow, by any means possible. It breathes in the amniotic fluid along with sensations. In it, desire and need are confused, they are entangled. This is slightly different from the situation of older patients who have already learned language. There, psychoanalysts learn to distinguish among need, desire, and the request.

For a psychoanalyst working with newborns and taking an interest in prenatal life, the body and language, desire and need, are the same thing. The child's body is born into several articulations of language. On the one hand, he enters a language bath constituted by the generations that preceded him: his parents' plan for a child, the spoken and unspoken words that preside over his conception, but also traumas going back to earlier generations. Note in that respect that the story of the baby blues is filled with allusions to an aunt, a grandparent, and so on. These allusions, repeatedly reshuffled among the successive members of the family line, bring questions to a head in the cries of baby blues, manifesting the hole of language that until then had served as a response. But, on the other hand, when the child herself acquires the so-called mother tongue, she will simultaneously grasp the *potential space of language,* in Lucien Kokh's terms, that is, a space of language where at least three generations are already in conversation.

The problem arises when that confusion between need and desire persists after birth, because no parental word has come to replicate the physiological cutting of the umbilical cord. It is then that the infant's cannibalistic oral drives can be triggered. It is extremely important to signify to the infant the difference between desire and need; otherwise, psychosis may set in. On this matter, Dolto cited the example of a child who, though delightful, bit everything within reach. He was kicked out of institutions, stores, parks, and so on, because, despite his sharp intelligence, he was a public menace. Dolto explained that she understood what was going on with that child when she saw his mother breastfeeding his younger brother. She fed him in silence, and by way of speaking to him, she constantly pinched and pawed at every part of his body. In a word, she created mouths over his entire body, she nursed him, cannibalized him, with her touch. The mother did not distinguish between the child's need for nourishment and the pleasure of sucking; she chained him to a "loving violence," which Dolto summed up in a phrase addressed to the child: "She needed to touch you and you thought that was good; and you believed that, when someone loves others, he must bite them and eat them."[4] Discouraging mothers from caressing their babies while feeding them is obviously not at issue. On the contrary. One must simply emphasize the importance of the loving words that usually accompany nursing.

Some researchers say that the role of the baby blues is to break the fusion between the mother and child; in this, they rely on an analogy with a prenatal fusion that does not, in fact, exist. Since there is a fusion between the fetus and the womb, they argue, there might be a fusion between one newborn or another and his mother, when she gets too close to him by her cuddling, her confidences, her imaginary proximity to him. We have already disposed of the notion of fetus-mother fusion, but let us return to it with a note: As soon as the placenta takes control of the pregnancy through the placental hormones, the mother and child have already broken their fusion. This occurs during the fourth month after conception. In the first days, the only thing happening is the multiplication of cell mitosis; on the fourth or fifth day, the first cellular differentiation occurs, and the egg migrates to the uterus. It is the implantation in the uterus of that morula, that little fertilized egg, that will lead a week later to the appearance of the trophoblast and the chorionic villi. The trophoblast, manufactured by the child as a temporary measure and precursor to the placenta, is already an intermediary between the fetus and the mother. Hence, there is an intermediary only because there is an exchange between the mother and the child. In no case is there any justification for saying they are one. It is through that "placental mouth" that the child breathes, feeds itself, and touches the mother.

Others, like psychoanalyst Serge Lebovici during a television broadcast, interpret the idea of fusion as follows: "I know of no baby except in the arms of its mother." By that, they mean that the sensations of the two are connected. They rely on an undeniable clinical reality: the baby, in the first days, choruses the emotions of her mother. But that hypersensitivity gradually diminishes. The intensity of these echoes weakens, without ever disappearing altogether. All the same, must we say they are one? The baby blues are there to permit us to assert, on the contrary, that it is the words addressed to the baby that give her her autonomy. In giving meaning to her emotions, these words and the desires they convey allow her to "think" them. Thereby, they establish the child in her dimension as an autonomous desiring subject, determined to confront her own future.

Gérard, a Newborn in Mourning

If the fetus has any desire, it is to live. He succeeds beyond one's greatest hopes: the pediatrician Marie Thirion remarked that 950 children out of 1,000 are born normal and healthy. An extraordinary rate if one thinks about it. She assumes this is possible only thanks to an exchange, a strong communication with the mother: "To live after birth, in an exact resemblance to the very first days after fertilization, when her implantation in the uterus immediately determined her survival or elimination, a newborn must take root in something living, must implant herself in a human relationship."[5]

Nevertheless, childbirth modifies that relationship, physiologically of course, but also psychically. It represents a radical break as well as a leap into the unknown. In other words, a mother's eventual anxiety is not transmitted in the same way after birth as before, if only because the newborn's response more easily modifies the mother's behavior in return. It is said that the newborn is defenseless, naked before life. What is striking above all is that he offers no resistance to what is coming from the outside. That is noticeable in the way he receives interpretations. It is not that he is more or less permeable than an older child, but that he offers practically no obstacle to these interpretations.

People are therefore astonished at the radical and dazzling effect of the interpretations, and they speak of magic. Magic has no place in the sudden changes experienced by these newborns who, within a few hours, may abandon the symptom that threatened them, including, sometimes, their vital functions. We must imagine that, in the psychoanalysis of adults, the memory work takes longer because of the many "layers" to be passed through. Some seriously neurotic adults have, in this regard, been amputated from thought and from exchanges. Their history is made up of paltry words, missing words, of strata that constitute walls they have bumped up against in an almost corporeal sense of the term. They have thus developed a certain number of defenses, reaction formations against their own capacity for exchange and thought, which have led to their suffering. Lost in the strata of their history, they need time to recover their trust in the words of the other, and hence in their own words. Nevertheless, they remain wholly sensitive to the almost corporeal articulation of their troubles. The problem is how to gain access to that sensitivity.

It is more quickly accessible in the newborn, since there are fewer strata. They exist nevertheless, since the three-day-old baby was not born yesterday; he has a past of nearly nine months behind him. His symptom, when it exists, may be the deferred effect of an event that took place before birth: a fetal pathology or a prenatal shock, for example. But the newborn more quickly understands what allows him to come to symbolic life.

I learned that in part from a boy named Gérard, who spent his first forty-eight hours of life crying in his incubator in the kangaroo unit. These cries were worrisome, and an attending physician, who rarely turned to me for help under ordinary circumstances, insisted on pointing him out to me, along with the baby's mother, Mrs. Ruyckert, who seemed to be in great pain. She thus suggested to Mrs. Ruyckert that I intervene, and I had a talk with her and Gérard at her request.

In that conversation, she first told me about her pregnancy, a desired pregnancy: twins, a daughter and a son (Gérard), had been conceived without medical intervention. The Ruyckerts "divided up" their children in advance: the daughter for her, the son for him. Mrs. Ruyckert chose a name for "hers," Mr. Ruyckert for "his." She called her daughter "my little girl" and her son "the other one." But a delay in the little girl's intrauterine development was quickly detected, and she had to be followed closely. Mrs. Ruyckert's morale was not greatly affected, since she chose not to know the risk involved. If there was proper monitoring, she thought, everything would turn out for the best. She simply caressed her belly a great deal in the place her daughter was, to comfort her. When the patient finally had to be hospitalized in the high-risk pregnancy unit, it was discovered that the little girl had died in utero seven-and-a-half months into the pregnancy. Doctors performed an emergency amniocentesis in an attempt to understand the reason for the death. The examination revealed that the amniotic fluid was an off color, which suggested there might be an infection that could endanger the health of the surviving child. The doctors, who did not want to take any risks with that second child, immediately performed a cesarean section on

Mrs. Ruyckert. So it was that Gérard was born, at a birth weight that justified his being admitted to the kangaroo unit and placed in an incubator.

"Nothing can console me," she told me, "she was my daughter, she's dead forever. The other one, he's crying too, but he can't know what that represents for me."

During the session, I directed this woman toward her maternal family line. I learned that Mrs. Ruyckert's grandmother, Gérard's great-grand-mother, was also a twin. That woman found herself a widow with four children at a young age, without many resources, and the children endured a harsh upbringing. Mrs. Ruyckert even said her mother had been abused. For that grandmother, there was only enough to go around for male children. Only the boys went to school, and the girls had to serve them. Logically, then, her mother was placed as a house servant at a very young age in order to feed the family. The head of the household, who had lost his wife, seduced her and got her pregnant. That child, whom the father acknowledged, was Mrs. Ruyckert herself. A son soon followed; he was idolized, and Mrs. Ruyckert was pushed to the background. The first part of her adult life was nothing but emotional instability and conflicts with her mother, until she met and married Mr. Ruyckert, again a man "from a different social circle."

Even before commenting on that destiny, worthy of a Dickens novel, I thought it indispensable and urgent to explain things to Gérard: "You will never again see your sister, who was with you in your mother's belly; you can only keep her in your heart. She was not born alive, but you chose to be born and to live."

I spoke that way to the child about the mourning he had

to perform for his sister, because the things that happen without being expressed sometimes lead to fatal confusions. The fact that Gérard was grieving his sister was conceivable, but that he was inconsolable could not be explained unless one imagined that the sadness came from elsewhere and was waiting to be named.

I told Mrs. Ruyckert that it seemed to me that she had imposed on her daughter, who had all the advantages, the responsibility of avenging and making amends for the wrong done to the two despised women of the previous generations. I added a joke in the form of a counterwish: the fact that her eldest child was a boy undoubtedly lifted the burden from the daughter she might later have, that of warding off the curse on eldest daughters in the family. She seemed to find that interpretation to her taste, and ended the conversation with a question: What should be done with the body of the dead fetus? She would have considered burying or cremating it only if the baby had been born alive and then quickly died. But in this case? She had inscribed the child's name in the family record book, but that did not solve the problem raised by the body.

I received news a few days later. Notwithstanding the issue of what to do with the dead child's body, Gérard and his mother were thriving. A few questions remained for me, however. Deep down, I wondered whether the twin girl did not die from the enormity of that weight upon her: Had she sacrificed herself on the altar of the family neurosis? What desire for life on the part of the fetus, subjected to the mother's history, was so affected as to be unable to grow sufficiently or to be born? If the moral principle of the fetus is to live, what about those that give up along the way? I did not confide any of that to this woman. The effect would have been only to revive a sense of guilt that the conversation rightly attempted to contain, the same guilt that comes with most deaths in utero and premature births, and which leads mothers to say: "I did not succeed in bringing him to term!" There is a necessary step between birth and symbolic life, and that step must be accompanied by words. After childbirth comes the birth of the subject. That is the crucial moment of the baby blues.

The moment to become a subject certainly depends on the newborn. But it also depends on her parents and on the moment when they can empower her to be herself. Until then, the child is in an unsettled situation. The reality of birth has taken place and has dealt her a hard blow, but she has not yet got back on her feet, so to speak. Almost all children, let us note, are relatively quiet and calm until then. They sleep and recover from their emotions. It is a period of limbo: "I am no longer in my mother's womb, but I am not yet altogether among you; give me time." They are there, but they are still elsewhere. Then the baby blues occur: The mother's milk comes in, along with her tears; the child's phonic modulations burst forth; and the deferred effect of birth awakens them both to a new life. Remember Karina, who was so afraid of being born; she remained in the limbo of an incomplete birth because she lacked the support parental security would have provided.

Of course, every child has his own personality. Some babies have their eyes wide open, curious as they are about what is going on around them. Others, on the contrary, will keep their eyes shut for a time, preferring no doubt not to know too much about what is being said "outside." Nevertheless, that period of limbo, half one thing, half another, that moment of being in sleep that precedes the baby blues, is clinically observable.

Baby Blues, Mommy Blues, Daddy Blues

The act that the baby blues comes to sanction is on the order of castration, precisely what Dolto called "umbilical castration" (she sometimes also spoke of "fetal castration"). It is when the child awakens and the mother begins to cry that the replication of the cutting of the umbilical cord that took place three or four days earlier occurs.

BABY BLUES

This time, that symbolic cut affects the child as much as it depends on the parents. Inasmuch as that umbilical castration has been inscribed for the parents, inasmuch as they can recognize the newborn as someone who is not solely the fruit of their flesh, they will allow that child to gain access to the paternal metaphor: "You are the child born of our desire, as each of us was of our own parents, and so on back into the mists of time. Your life is marked by that history, it is now up to you to distance yourself from that history while at the same time honoring it, to make it into a singular and unprecedented life: your own."

That presupposes, on the parents' part, the acceptance of an implacable loss, which is not necessarily easy. When it is not possible, the child pays the price with his psychic health: He then remains in the place of the symptom. It is as if the parents, rather than inscribing the child's body in a symbolic sense, preferred that it remain within the real. In the no-man's-land of limbo, the newborn is caught between his real birth and his advent into the symbolic. In anticipating a first affirmation of his being-among-others, he is, as it were, awaiting the judgment of Solomon, born but not yet *other* in the eyes of his parents.

I spoke of symbolic birth at the time of the baby blues. The imaginary child, I said, can cohabit with the real child of flesh, without threatening him. There is no need to mourn him. If there is a mourning for the mother to perform, it is of the fetus and the pregnancy, and their "replacement" with a new mother-child relationship under the purview of the father and his name. This explains why a mother says, at the most profound point of her depression: "Before, I got all the attention. Now it's the baby who gets all the attention." These mothers experience themselves as the waste product, the remainder of a division in the algebraic sense. The mother is confronted with something that surpasses her on all sides: The child goes from being real to being symbolic, and the distance is difficult to overcome.

When, on the fourth day, the child begins to use her voice for the purpose of communication, this is a symbolization, a *realization,* as psychoanalyst Wilfred Bion would say. The child's modulations are concrete expressions corresponding to a stimulation, an awakening, of the brain; they are phonic realizations. With the infant's phonatory realization comes a cerebralization of the forms his gestures and bodily functions take. These are two parallel functions. On one hand, the infant reacts cerebrally to sounds, spoken words potentially charged with meaning that are exchanged between him and those around him; he reacts, in the first place, to those of his mother, of whom he is the first body graft. On the other hand, his bodily functions mirror oral expression.

This can lead to confusion. For example, some theorists think of oral language as crude, and think that written language is the natural refuge for concepts and thought. That goes against what is understood among newborns. The infant, a child of language, is a thinker: He reacts as a function of the reactions around him. His emotions/sensations are not simply affects, but the first modalities of his capacity to think. Conversely, as Dolto noted, in infants separated early from their mothers, infants for whom no words signified the birth, one observes "language delays and defects, speech impediments that make pronouncing all or some phonemes impossible. There are cries that are continual expulsions of sounds, or, on the contrary, a total absence of voicing because of a symbolic absence in the larynx, the place of active pleasure for modulating communication."

MOMMY BLUES

On the mother's side, castration consists of realizing she is dealing with a true human being, a baby subject. She must feel she is in the position of a service provider who is thanked with a smile for the tremendous labor accomplished, then later thanked, period, without a smile, because she is no longer needed. This is the moment she realizes that, though she is the child's maker, she is not the only one. Her child's body was a lodger in her own, but she is not its owner. It takes her time to think through that gap between her and the child.

FROM BIRTH TO LIFE'S LIMBO 171

This is the time of limbo, and of the baby blues that bring it
to its conclusion.

This requires a renunciation on her part, since she can no
longer fail to recognize that the child's future belongs by
rights to him. She will of course influence his development,
but he will have already begun to make a place for himself.
Her ability to acknowledge the place he has taken depends on
the place that was set aside for her when she was very young.
Was she or was she not permitted to situate herself as *other,* as
a singular individual, in her family line? It is often that question that returns to center stage with the baby blues.

That problem of the place to be taken by the baby has a
physical dimension for newborns who do not manage to gain
weight after a few days. That problem seems to recur as an
echo of the mother's inability to find a place for herself after
her own birth. That is the reason why the baby blues so often
vanish as soon as we can speak to the mother about her relationship to her own mother.

I am thinking of a woman I met during her two deliveries, of her first child, Joseph, and then of her daughter, Laure,
the following year. For the first child, she was in despair about
not being able to breastfeed. For her, that thwarted desire
to breastfeed stemmed from an unconscious obligation she
felt not to follow her mother's example. Her own mother, in
fact, had not breastfed any of her five children, and professed
a fierce opposition to breastfeeding. Some time after the
birth, the couple wanted to make the baptism a large family
celebration. They had cause to regret it, since the celebration
turned into a display of family dramas. The woman's younger
brother refused to come to the party, and their mother made
the daughter pay for her younger brother's defection, by put-

ting on a long face that was hardly appropriate. As she told me this, the woman realized that she had been cast aside in favor of her brother throughout her childhood, something she had always tried to ignore. Of course, everyone makes the best of misfortunes to acquire a surplus of hope, and this woman used that opportunity to get closer to her father, especially after her parents' separation. It was certainly that regard for the paternal and masculine image that later helped her have a successful marriage. But the problem of jealousy remained central, and appeared in the form of an extreme agitation and irritability when her second child arrived. She could not bear the idea that jealousy might arise between her two children. Her agitation stemmed from the fact that she was constantly thinking up strategies to avoid in advance any distance between them: Should she take her son out of daycare so that he would know she was devoting as much attention to him as to the newborn? Did she have to be discreet when cuddling the younger child, so as not to upset the older one? And so on. Clearly, in continuing to favor Joseph, she was mounting little resistance to the repetition drive, which made her take the same position in relation to her first two children as her mother had taken toward her and her brother. Her mother, in her omnipotence, undoubtedly did not foresee the possibility that her elder daughter would become a mother in turn. To manage that, her daughter had to commit three successive transgressions. First, she had to give birth, and that was already a challenge to the mother's omnipotence. In fact, the woman started over three times, since three spontaneous miscarriages had preceded Joseph's birth. Second, she had to be able to breastfeed, against the view professed by her mother; that was at the heart of her baby blues when the first child was born. Third, she had to accept, in her mother's place, the daughter as an equal to her son; that was the unsolved problem that Laure's arrival raised for her.

A Place Too Small for Anne

Mrs. Rigaud asked to see me one day because she was crying a great deal. She was the mother of triplets: Anne had been sent to the neonatal ward because she weighed only one pound, five ounces; Maxime and Nathalie were hospitalized beside their mother in the kangaroo unit, because they were slightly underdeveloped. She was rightly worried about the pain Anne's breathing tube was causing, since, at the time I saw her, there was little pain relief protocol in the treatment of premature babies. But the mother's crying had not let up for two days, despite the visits she was able to make to Anne and the reassurance given her that the prognosis was not overly unfavorable for the immediate future.

I was welcomed into the room by Mr. and Mrs. Rigaud, and by Nathalie and Maxime, who were in their incubators. As Mrs. Rigaud remarked to me, "There are as many people here as this room can hold, and yet one is missing."

The story she told me of the birth of her triplets was full of digressions. Six years earlier, the couple had had a first daughter, Maud; that birth brought on a postpartum depression in Mrs. Rigaud that lasted six months. A five-year period of infertility followed. Treatment for that infertility was undertaken at Béclère and, after five years, artificial insemination resulted in a pregnancy. When the couple learned during the second week of gestation that there were three embryos present, they thought an embryonic reduction was being prescribed. This is an operation intended to destroy in situ one of the embryos and hence to increase the remaining embryos' chances of survival. It is a delicate procedure, and doctors feel some uneasiness in performing it: Although the selection of the embryo to be taken is not exactly the luck of the draw, it does raise certain problems of conscience. That is why, with the advent of that technique, the ethical reflections conducted by René Frydman and his team imposed a dual imperative. On principle, reduction is not considered at Béclère except for pregnancies of at least quadruplets, and it must be proposed to the couples, never imposed on them. In Mrs. Rigaud's case, the experience unfolded at another institution, and there was a misunderstanding. Believing she was being prescribed embryonic reduction as a medical treatment, she fell into a depression, and the couple anticipated grieving one of the embryos. When, after a more extensive discussion, the parents were assured that their agreement was required, they rejected the reduction and decided to bring all three fetuses to term.

Upon hearing that, I suggested to Mrs. Rigaud that she go see Anne in intensive care and explain that imbroglio to her. At least Anne should hear from her mother that the grief and depression at the beginning of the pregnancy did not correspond to her parents' desire to get rid of one of their children; she should know they did not require that she occupy the place of a victim, in a sacrifice they did not want. She should also hear from her mother's mouth the reason for the treatment and for her suffering.

I saw her again three days later and learned that, scarcely

a few hours after her parents spoke to Anne, the tubes were removed and she was able to breathe on her own for twelve hours. Mrs. Rigaud, whose husband was absent on my second visit, told me about her depression during her first pregnancy. She had a very hard time dealing with the behavior of her in-laws at the time of the first birth. Until then, they had idolized her, but all of a sudden Maud was getting all the attention and she was now considered little more than a surrogate mother.

Then she made associations relating to her own birth. Like her daughter Anne, she was the fourth child in the family. She knew she was not wanted and that, moreover, her parents would have preferred a boy. His name was all picked out—Paul—and her parents' disappointment was such that they did not come up with a name for her until three days later. Her reaction was very clear and decided her future for a long time. She became a good girl, did everything she could not to be a bother and to be accepted. When she became an adult, she made a point of proving herself, as her professional success attested. She also devoted that success to her family, since Mrs. Rigaud had supported them financially since that time. The birth of her first daughter, and the behavior of her in-laws, who in some sense were asking her to again efface herself, thus revived the memory of that place that was never her own—"there are as many people as there is room for, and yet someone is missing." Since, fortunately, she was not altogether the good girl she had been before becoming a mother, all she could do was grieve the birth of her daughter, and her own birth. To punctuate that second conversation, I advised the mother to tell all that to her daughter Anne, who also seemed to be effacing herself so as not to be a bother: to tell her who she was in relation to her siblings and the family line, what her own place was.

We saw each other again for a third conversation, at which time I received confirmation that Anne was doing better, that she now weighed more than two pounds and was drinking her mother's milk. Maxime and Nathalie were able to leave their incubators, and Mrs. Rigaud had recovered her enjoyment of things. But it was now Mr. Rigaud's turn to become depressed and brittle. He could no longer bear to visit Anne with his wife or to talk to her. It had reached the point that Mrs. Rigaud was concealing things from him, and she added that he was behaving as if he were her fifth child. Maxime, as his mother was speaking about the father, commented emphatically on the conversation. I then offered to see the father, but she assured me he would refuse, since he already believed it was unwarranted for me to have meddled in their lives. She added that she felt responsible, since she had carefully omitted to inform him of our first conversation. I better grasped why he was taken aback by my "intrusion." I therefore offered to write the father to clear up that misunderstanding, an idea to which she readily agreed. In the letter, I told Mr. Rigaud that I never would have allowed myself to intervene in their lives without his consent and without the provision that he be informed. Five days later, the father read the message without a word in front of his wife; doing demonstrably better, he again went to Anne's bedside with his wife.

Anne, for her part, had not gotten out of her difficulties. She developed laryngeal spasms as soon as anyone tried to remove her breathing tube; if the tube was left in place, she breathed calmly, without the ventilator. Anne was still ambivalent. Remembering the calendar, I advised the mother to tell her daughter: "We have now reached the date when you would normally have arrived, had you been carried to term. If that had been the case, you would then have breathed on your own, without the help of a machine. I understand you would like me to rock you, caress you, and feed you, but I can't so long as that machine is connected to you. As soon as possible, I'll do that with pleasure. I'll also give you a piece of cloth I've worn so that you always have my smell near you, and I'll come to see you often and talk to you to support you, until we're reunited."

It occurred to me that, for Anne, this tube might be an equivalent of the umbilical cord that connected her to a lost placenta, and that it now was taking the place of her mother, who, by necessity, was not present enough. Was I right or wrong? I don't know, there wasn't time to say. Mrs. Rigaud, Maxime, and Nathalie left the hospital very soon after that. A few weeks later, Anne was able to do without the breathing tube, and rejoined them at home.

I learned much later that new problems arose subsequently, which required several hospitalizations. Anne stopped fighting at the end of her first year and died. Analysis cannot do everything; all the same, I hope it was able to ease the harshness of her life.

When depression sets in and becomes chronic, the problem often goes back to something connected to the grandparents on one side or the other. The context of the mother's or father's birth returns to the surface. The child is, in fact, the concrete realization of the mother's paternal and maternal lines (and of the father's as well, in fact). Through the memories of the child's progenitors, the living and the dead appear between the lines: what is said about them and what is left out, the tribute that is paid or not paid to the dead in the family. The child displays all that in abridged form. She is the result both of the woman's potential for motherhood within the framework of these family lines and of her alliance with a man, the child's father, and with his lineage. It is up to the mother, through castration, to give up considering the child only as the fruit of her womb. It is that castration of the mother that makes the child's symbol-producing castration possible. As is well recognized, that castration is a positive movement: It has to do with the child's place in the family lines, and therefore transcends the process of naming the child (selecting a name, summoning witnesses, and so on). It is in that sense that the baby blues, in spite of the difficult times they entail, have the liberating effect of breathing life into the child.

DADDY BLUES

What about the fathers? They face castration as well. The fathers are walking on air, but that joy is not without its price. Let us cite René Frydman, at once a husband, a father, and an obstetrician. The scene takes place at a café. His wife was soon to give birth, and he was to meet her there.

"Someone calls me on the phone: 'Your wife is having a baby, you have to come.' I arrive at the hospital, look around, and ask: 'Have you seen Mrs. Frydman? She must be at the very start of her labor.'

" 'Yes, everything's fine, it's a boy, do you want to see him?'

"Straightaway they bring me some little fellow. I have angina for three days."[6]

A father may get angina, but he may also get the baby blues, in his own way. Men cry less, it is true, under these circumstances, but they reel from the blow in their manner: an unexplained bout of fatigue, forgotten appointments, driving errors, and more or less serious accidents on the way to the maternity ward. People have spoken with a great deal of irony about the syndrome known as "couvade," a behavior of African fathers, who are granted the right, after their wives have given birth, to stay in bed and remain isolated and inactive for a certain time. There is less tolerance for that kind of ritualized behavior in our postindustrial societies. But, since the human being is never without resources, equivalents have been found in my country and, in this regard, they put the two parents on equal footing.

What is at stake? Is it the same baby blues for a father as for a mother? Not altogether. The situation is difficult for the father. Until then, he may have had the impression that he did not play a very great role in his child's uterine development; and now this little thing is demanding all the attention. Already, in some cases, he is cast aside at the time of birth because "it's women's business," or because it's the business of doctors; to add to that, no one is paying attention to him now. He may come to have doubts: *mater certa, pater incertus* (the mother is always the mother, the father is uncertain). In any case, he is not yet in a position to be fully acknowledged as a father. It is assumed that he is the "happy father" no doubt, but the mother has not really had the time to authenticate him as such in relation to their child. He may display some annoyance. And he may not arrive at the maternity ward in time for "the blessed event." He has little problems, as they say: a bad flu, car trouble. But you never know where little worries will lead you. It's a thin line between the comic and the tragic, and you're never sure you've seen the worst of it.

So it happened that, arriving to see a new mother in her room where she was waiting for me, I found her husband in the bed with a cast from his thigh to his toes, and his wife seated at his bedside to assist him. This was probably the most unexpected sight I ever chanced upon in a maternity ward. It seems this man had had a bad fall the day of the birth. He had to be hospitalized, and so he was brought to visit his wife and child by ambulance.

He was not the only one, in any case, to be violently affected by the birth, since the mother spent time in the high-risk pregnancy unit during her seventh month of pregnancy because of a risk of premature delivery. That hospitalization gave the woman a great deal to think about during our conversation, and seemed to persuade her to enter psychoanalysis in the future. In addition, she was displaying a bad case of baby blues, complicated by the fact that her daughter had had to be placed in the kangaroo unit for respiratory troubles. A diagnostic evaluation was thus being done to learn what the problem was.

Our conversation brought to light the major transgression that the child's birth represented. The mother had had to brave the most brutal family prohibitions to give birth after the age of forty, and, in that respect, the birth was almost like an act of violence. We may suppose that is how the mother understood it. She told me that, in speaking to me, she became aware of how heavy these prohibitions weighed on their shoulders as parents, and even more on her daughter's shoulders. She now saw her daughter's symptoms as an appeal made to her parents for them to take care of her. It was as if, she said, her daughter were asking them to set aside the family quarrels in order to create a new family unit with her.

The father reacted to his wife's words like a man, like the father he had become thanks to the two of them. He took the child in his arms and gave her the bottle, slowly, delicately, in a silence filled with intense emotion, which enveloped the three protagonists. I could even say the four of us, since I was very touched to see that father, lying in his wife's bed, giving the bottle to their child for the first time, and letting his tears flow.

The problem with these "accidents" is that they lead the fathers to an authentic regression to childhood, at the level of their bodies. Infections, flu, angina, colds, sprains, fractures, even appendicitis or renal colic requiring hospitalization— anything can be used to put the father in the position of a child who must be taken care of, while another, real child is monopolizing his wife's attention. For fathers, castration consists of getting rid of the image of their own mothers to whom they are attached. They too can be induced to talk about their own birth and the place made for them.

Few things in our society are designed to support fathers after the birth of a child. This is a moment of potential fragility for them, since, though they are certainly considered the progenitors of their child, they are not yet seen as fathers in the full sense of the term. There are too rarely brothers, cousins, and in-laws in the community around them, as is the case in other types of social organization. As a result, it is not clear whether the signs of suffering by these fathers who get the baby blues are taken seriously enough.

The child's birth owes something to a father, and to a mother, and to something more. That something, which has to do with the word and the symbolic, will come to pass provided the child can recognize himself as an independent being of desire, with all questions of physiological maturity and social autonomy set aside. In that birth to himself, the primary thing is the connection to the other—specifically, to his mother and what she will transmit to him about the name and function of the father in relation to her. That connection is established in postnatal life on the basis of the mother's renunciation of the child as a lump of flesh that is simply a continuation of herself. It is understood that that castration is an ordeal for her, as the baby blues demonstrate. But the ordeal is also a salvation for her, for the newborn, and for the child's father.

6. Confidential Childbirth: The Child Given Up at Birth

"A secret always has the shape of an ear." —JEAN COCTEAU

There are newborns who do not have the luxury of sharing the strange problems of baby blues with their mothers. These are children left by their mothers to the care of an institution that will rear them from birth until an adoptive family welcomes them. Of course, unlike the baby blues, what in France is called confidential childbirth is rare: between five hundred and seven hundred cases per year, depending on the estimate. Nevertheless, it too is in need of the word that affects the limbo period.

To make light of things for a moment, we may say that children resulting from confidential childbirth have the good luck not to have to deal with the expectations and imaginary projections of those who conceived them: "My child should have been a boy, and it's only a girl"; "My child will have my nose and will study the fine arts like her mother"; and so on. That can help them. Dolto has even claimed that it immediately places them in the situation of analysis: "From the moment we [analysts] have to enter into a relationship with a child who no longer has her birth parents . . . we can tell her that she is her own parents. In representing the primal scene all by herself, she is, in fact, in the situation of a subject; . . . if she will work with us, she will be, in her place as a subject, much more liberated than other children."[1]

Let us add that, in the case of newborns, the effects of being a subject from the outset are spectacular: They very often promise a good beginning, if, and only if, the newborns' stories are told to them. Indeed, although these newborns no longer have their parents to influence them, they hold them in their hearts (*internal parents,* in Dolto's expression), and their absence is cruelly felt. Since the time I spent observing Dolto's practice, I have seen a number of children resulting from confidential birth in a grave state of distress.

I have indicated how, for these two reasons—these children's extreme pain and their extraordinary capacity to emerge from it—I made the decision to work in the maternity ward. It was thanks to them that I became convinced that a psychoanalyst ought to go listen to newborns and speak to them. It is to them that I am indebted for thinking that a baby can die from a lack of words. It is they who impel me to bear witness today.

Was it possible to act in such a way that, very early on, at their birth, children could already understand an account of their "life from before" (the separation), even though none of the representatives of their story (father, mother, and so on) were there any longer to tell them? It was these children, who no longer had any connection to their parents or their family line, who made it particularly interesting for me to go to the maternity ward to speak to newborns who were not thriving. These children, because they were unable to situate their short history "transgenerationally," could not attribute any meaning to their life to come, and an attempt had to be made to intervene and help them do it.

Confidential childbirth represents an exception to a psychoanalyst's usual work: first, because, fortunately, it affects only a small proportion of newborn patients; and second, because it falls within the category of a speech emergency.

A psychoanalyst is not accustomed to emergencies; she is rather wary of them, as a trap that would prevent her from hearing that the unconscious has no notion of time. Nevertheless, an emergency intervention is necessary in the case of a confidential childbirth. Care adapted to these children given up by their parents is certainly necessary, and institutions are now applying themselves more or less successfully to providing it. But, in addition to that, they need a true welcome in language if they are to thrive. One must act, as quickly and as effectively as possible, to give a name to things and allow these children to take on their humanity; it has too often happened that neglect in this regard, combined with the pain of separation, has nearly made them lose it.

From X to Exette

In this case, naming the human can be taken literally. Hence, near the beginning of my practice in the maternity ward, I once ran into a neonatal aide carrying, as she often did, a baby "kangaroo style"; that is, wrapped in an apron against her belly to maintain constant contact with her. She came toward me: "Let me introduce you to Exette!"

"Exette? That's her name?"

"Well ... She was born anonymously, as Baby X, four days ago, and since she has no name, we call her Exette in the meantime."

Exette? How could anyone at a cutting-edge maternity ward accept the idea that a newborn, alone without her mother on the ward, should be called such a thing? "X" by way of identification. And "-ette" to indicate the sex: hardly more than an anonymous female! What kind of a society would put up with such symbolic violence?

I left to make inquiries, and I learned that the mother had not wanted to give the child a name. As is customary in such cases, it was the midwife who assigned one to her: Sandra. Thereupon, the bureau of public records ordered the name withdrawn, on the pretext that the midwife had no right to name the child. Hence that makeshift nickname, Exette, as everyone awaited the next municipal injunction. As it happened, that "legal" intervention was not only unknowingly violent, but was also invalid vis-à-vis the law at the time. It was very quickly rescinded, at our request, by a letter from the district attorney, since it was based on a confusion. That "error" certainly had its logic, but was no less "crazy" for all that. City hall based the error on the fact that it alone had the right to "assign names to children whose filiation is unknown." But a child whose filiation is kept confidential is not a child whose filiation is unknown. It therefore took only a few telephone calls to set things right and to return Sandra's name to her.

I then set out to uncover the little that was known of her story, and I invited the neonatal aide to accompany me when

I spoke to the baby. "Your name is Sandra," I began, then recounted her life to her. During the time that short exposition lasted, she physically reacted with an expression I have not forgotten. She kept opening and closing her mouth as if she were swallowing what I was saying. I was moved by that "response" and, at the end of the conversation, the neonatal aide said: "Thank you for her!" This was not a simple sucking reflex on the baby's part, but a physical incorporation of the words, and, on our part, an equally physical sensation of being listened to.

If I might have believed I was the victim of sentimentality, the repetition of such expressions from a number of newborns given up by their parents has silenced my fear. I am grateful for the history of psychoanalysis, which produced concepts such as incorporation at the oral stage linked to identification, and notions such as symbolic nourishment. They allow us to grasp that the subject thinks, "cobbles together" concepts, and that these concepts are in the first place of the body. In this case, they consisted of a turned-up mouth in a child who began to smile at the life she was seizing; and of an understanding, in the neonatal nurse, of that child's situation through her belly in contact with her.

From One Separation to Another

The fate of these children born without a name is unknown to me. But, before any eventual adoption, the future of children resulting from a confidential birth consists of repeated separation and of waiting.

First, of course, there is the separation from the mother

at birth. But there is also the departure from the hospital to a state nursery, a temporary foster family, or a mother's helper; there is another break when the child joins an adoptive family. These repeated rifts with the surroundings reactualize the child's first separation. It is from these findings that I began. The symptoms displayed by some of these babies referred back to connections created with those who had taken care of them in the first days of their lives at the hospital. Because these connections were not symbolized, nor was the inevitable separation that put an end to them, the rift reappeared as a clinical symptom.

It is therefore necessary to explain to the children the limits of these connections, to tell them they are only temporary, that the neonatal nurses are not their mothers but people paid to take care of them. We must add that separation from them is not a piece of their story that keeps repeating itself, but an important stage and a departure for a new institution where their future is being planned: a future adoption, for example, but also any type of future based on a social connection, and not on the inevitability of an ever-repeated separation.

For a newborn separated from his mother and wandering from hospital to institution while waiting to be adopted, to leave is sometimes to be so unattached to one's life as to endure it without wanting to play a role in it. In all the literature associated with early separation, the most diverse symptoms have been described. Various theories have come to light to explain them, the most famous still being that of *attachment,* which, as I said in chapter 2, I do not embrace. But, whatever the options, these beings, for whom childhood spent in an institution, or even adoption, has proved problematic, are all children who were unable to put into place symbolically what they confusingly experienced through their perceptions at birth or before.

THE STATE OF THE LAW

Let us leave aside adoption, and concern ourselves with the principal reason for it: abandonment. That was the word used in the past. The law in France has banned its use, which it considers pejorative in nearly all cases. Therefore, the terms "anonymous birth," "nameless" birth, and, recently, "confidential childbirth," have been employed in succession.

In French society, a specific law allows women to give birth to a child without anyone having the legal right to state that the child is in fact hers. "Anyone" means the mayor or any representative of society as well as the medical staff that aided in the delivery, and the child himself. After a period of three days at most, the child must be taken from his mother and entrusted to a private or public institution for the purpose of adoption.

The secret of the birth is recorded in a file sent to the department of health and social services; in the best of cases, that file contains information about what the mother allows or does not allow to be said regarding the biological father's name and the circumstances of the birth. It may also include a message addressed to the child by the mother. In addition, there is a statement that the mother relinquishes her parental rights, signed by the social worker, not by the mother. The child, upon reaching legal age, may seek permission to consult the file and may discover, in principle, the part of the secret the mother agreed to share with him. If his adoptive parents agree to it and accompany him, he may even consult this file at age thirteen.

For a period of two months, the mother may change her mind and ask to have her child returned to her. After that, nothing a priori must stand in the way of a definitive separation.

As it stands, that law presupposes an excellent collaboration between the different partners who are dealing with the baby: social workers, hospital staff, public and private institutions dealing with adoption, and the appropriate governmental agencies. That is not always the case, but, since the experiment conducted by Dolto thirty years ago, relations between Children's Services, the Antony nursery, and the "shrinks" have been particularly sound and well worked out. Dolto received suffering children in her practice and retraced their histories based on the symptoms and the material they brought to the session. In the same way, with the representatives of Children's Services, she perfected a system aimed at keeping the children directly informed of the progress of their files. Representatives regularly came to see the children in the maternity ward, then at the Antony nursery, and described to them the status of the measures taken: "We're looking for a family for you," "We've found it," "There's a problem getting you one because you're sick," and so on. This system is still in place and allows for an extraordinary collaboration between the nursery and Health and Social Services or Children's Services. Nevertheless, the problem of urgency immediately arises. In fact, although Children's Services representatives come to the hospital as soon as they are informed of a confidential childbirth, the slightest delay or lack of organization undermines their desire to intervene quickly.

That delay can be as long as several weeks, during which time no one speaks to the babies. It is therefore absolutely essential that such glitches do not leave these children without recourse for such a long period of time: A means must be found to ensure them emergency words. That requires an effort of reflection on my part, which is shared with everyone, both the hospital staff and the various other partners.

Another time problem can arise at the hospital. Must the mothers be prohibited from going to see the child they have decided to give up so long as he is in the hospital, or should they be permitted to visit? At Béclère, to respect the mother's decision, we take the child away and place him in the pediatric ward. We nevertheless let the mother visit him whenever she wishes, provided she is accompanied by a social worker or a midwife who can guarantee she is truly the mother. No law expressly prohibits it. The staff in the pediatric ward also do not feel authorized to prohibit her from bathing or caring for the child. We explain to her, however, that she will no longer have access to her child once he has left the hospital. That is how we interpret the gray area of the law in this matter.

CONFIDENTIAL CHILDBIRTH:
ITS EFFECT ON STAFF

On the maternity ward, what is puzzling at first is the effect that a confidential childbirth has on the nursing staff in general. Confidential birth carries with it an aura of drama, and, in that respect, sets in motion personal behaviors charged with uncontrolled emotions, or even the reflexes of a citizen or voter: You're for or against it, you're glad about it or distressed, you'd like to prevent it or do something to see that it goes well. It is extremely difficult to keep a minimal neutrality, though this is desirable if one wants to avoid seeing mother and child tossed about by moral and ideological issues that are larger than they. There were many serious mistakes made in the maternity ward, and here again "laws" had to be set in place; that is, a particular protocol had to be established to check the uncontrolled effects of personal shortcomings. At the time, these mistakes led some staff members to reactions that, after the fact, they judged uncharacteristic of them, yet they were very real.

Once, a pediatrician on the maternity ward, as gifted in her professional seriousness as in her sensitive approach to "baby persons," had to accompany a child born confidentially to the pediatric ward, located at the other end of the hospital, where he would wait to be transferred to the state nursery. The child was of the same ethnic origin as the pediatrician and she was repelled at the unhappy fate she ascribed to him. During the trip between the two wards, strange and uncontrollable thoughts occurred to her, as she confided to me after the fact. She got it into her head to take the baby home with her and raise him with her own children. Without reasoning with herself any further, she spoke to him in her mind: "Poor little thing, I'm going to take you home, raise you with my own, so that you can have a good family."

That irresistible thought preoccupied her all through the corridors, and she was ready to turn her life upside down in an instant. But, as she told me subsequently, something indestructible in her body—was it her white physician's smock?—held her back and summoned her to run to the pediatric ward to join her colleagues and recover her senses.

This she did, happy to escape her first impulse. But since the most irresistible impulses are often the most tenacious, and the unconscious is not silenced by an "examination of conscience," she left behind a small trace of her first desire. Contrary to the fundamental safety principles of her profession, which she is the last to neglect, she forgot to indicate to her colleagues that the child's mother had diabetes, and that the baby's glycemia thus had to be controlled. Fortunately, the oversight was quickly identified and remedied, and the child was cared for as he ought to have been.

How is it that the most hardened professionals can deviate from their duties? While they are in the hospital, these "confidential" children, cut off from their mothers, find themselves in a no-man's-land, in a weightless state in the fantasyland of parental possibilities awakened in everyone. Everyone may feel called upon to be these children's parents, as it were. I do not say this feeling is necessarily conscious. Nevertheless, someone may, for an instant, give in to that imaginary appeal. The reactions are not necessarily "generous," however. They are often negative and rejecting, usually moralizing.

On one occasion, a mother who had given birth confidentially declined to see the baby. An intern of the same ethnic origin as she, who could not bear the idea that a woman from his community, which does not allow adoption, could give up her child, rushed to the delivery room and forcibly put the baby in her arms. He told her the child was magnificent, and that she ought to take a good look at him and hold him to her. Another time, an anesthesiologist judged a young mother who had given birth confidentially too common to understand how childbirth under an epidural would come to pass, and therefore judged he did not have to prescribe that type of anesthesia for her. Was she called upon to suffer as the price for giving up her child? I personally asked a midwife to intervene in that case to obtain what any woman would have had in a situation other than confidential childbirth, and the epidural was given.

Still another time, it was a public records official who took it upon himself to reject the name "Mohamed" from a mother who had given birth confidentially, because that name was too ethnic and "the poor child already had enough problems as it was." More agreeably, there was a nurse who continually called an abandoned baby she was taking care of "my poor little thing." How could the "poor little thing" fail to run into difficulties in its later efforts to be a human being, big and happy?

It is difficult to escape such inappropriate reactions, or at least criticisms of the intentions of women who ask to give birth confidentially. It was in part to relieve staff members of that agonizing or distressing weight that I gradually elaborated a procedure for dealing with the demands of confidential childbirth.

A SPEECH EMERGENCY: PIERRETTE'S JOURNEY

The case of Pierrette is sufficiently exemplary of the role played by "giving" in the act of "giving up" a child to take note of it here. It led me to reflect a great deal about the procedure for respectfully welcoming these women in distress.

Pierrette, age thirteen, slightly more than seven months pregnant, presented herself one day at Béclère, to give birth and to explain her situation. She was accompanied by her mother. At Pierrette's request, I saw them together.

They seemed very close, though, as yet, they knew each other very little. Pierrette had seen her parents only occasionally before age three, and then never again until now. Pierrette's mother was from sub-Saharan Africa and had come to France to study, along with her husband, when Pierrette was three months old. She entrusted her daughter to her sister in their native country. Three years after Pierrette's birth, the father was designated an opponent of the regime and was barred from returning home. Pierrette's brothers and sisters then found refuge in France, while Pierrette remained in sub-Saharan Africa in her aunt's care. Shortly before our conversation, the father had died of cardiac arrest. At that time, the mother finally obtained authorization to reunite the family, authorization that had been refused her until that time. It was owing to her father's death that Pierrette was able to return to her family. She therefore came to France.

During the medical exam required for immigration, Pierrette's pregnancy was discovered. She told me she was not aware of it at the time. In addition, she had only recently begun menstruating, and said she knew nothing about sex. According to her, it was the brother of a friend of hers who raped her. In any case, knowing she was pregnant, she left for France and there was reunited with her mother. When the mother was informed, she decided to accompany her daughter to Béclère. Given the situation, I set out the details of the problem and the different scenarios: an institution, a foster family, the eventuality that the child could be raised by its grandmother, confidential childbirth. I suggested they think things over and make another appointment, which they did.

By the second conversation, the response was ready, and they said it in chorus: "We're going to give it!"

A lovely gift in fact, all the more precious for being anonymous. Then each of them gave her reasons. Pierrette's mother explained she had weighed the pros and cons: "I might have liked to care for the child myself. If my husband were alive, that certainly would have been possible. But I am too deeply affected by grief, it is too soon for me to feel able to raise that child."

Pierrette was more laconic: "I'm thirteen years old and I can't be a mother. I want to go to school."

It was thus decided that the child would be entrusted to Children's Services. The child's future was discussed by the mother and grandmother. The mother refused to see him but promised "a prayer" for him. The grandmother, for her part, insisted on transmitting something. With her daughter's consent, she proposed to help her at the birth, and to give the child a first and middle name as well as a medallion. Rarely has the file for a confidential birth been so precise. After the birth, the grandmother and I went to speak to the child. Pierrette asked us to tell him everything except the matter of the rape and her identity. The child was magnificent. The grandmother, in tears, held him in her arms for the entire meeting. The two of us were able to tell the child about his father, the fact that he did not know about the birth, the absence of love accompanying his conception, his mother's hope that, conversely, he would find love in another family. The grandmother added all the touching wishes of which her generous heart was capable. The child left for the pediatric ward, then was taken in by the state nursery.

As is clear, I intentionally withheld any advice or evaluation. They play no role in the reception of women who ask to give birth confidentially. In these conversations, I never judge or encourage. I am content to remain firm about the procedure: "Nothing will be decided without you, in the strict sense of the term. We are here, the social worker and I, to clarify for you the possibilities the law grants you and the importance your cooperation will have for the child. I am here to honor your wishes and to give them the force of law. But it is up to you to make the decisions."

The moving journey of these two women during these conversations is, I hope, an eloquent plea for such an active neutrality. Of course, Pierrette was still a child, and it was as a child that she wanted to rid herself of her baby without concerning herself further. Of course, she may have been repeating the de facto abandonment of which she was victim at the age of three months. And of course, that "present" she was giving effaced something that, though she refused to admit it, would never truly be a present for her. But that present was truly a gift as much as a "giving up": It was discussed and spoken about between Pierrette and her mother.

Working with Confidential Childbirth: How I Developed My Procedures

To allow subjects in distress to go forward, I had to think about a general procedure that would allow me to listen to these mothers with respect for their pain, to support them, to work with them in the urgency their situation demanded, and to speak to their children.

When I arrived, it was the usual practice to send mothers asking for a confidential birth to one of the social workers. With them, we created a study group on the matter. The idea was to exchange ideas and to work with people in the maternity ward as well as the directors of the Antony nursery, which received the majority of the babies entrusted to Children's Services. Staff members from the maternity ward and pediatrics who felt it was their concern came to these meetings, regardless of their position. In addition, coming from outside the hospital were representatives of the Antony nursery, high-level supervisors from Children's Services and the adoption services, and some members of area organizations. These bimonthly meetings were intense and passionate. Everything was discussed, from the names to be given the children to the law in force, what one could and could not do, what remained ambiguous or hazy. For a time, discussions turned on the need to speak to newborns and to do so in an emergency capacity, and on the means that would make that aim realizable. Despite everyone's desire to collaborate in the name of the child's best interests, my practice was disputed by some, on the pretext that Family Counseling, the agency serving as legal guardian, was responsible for selecting what was to be said to the child as a function of "his own good," and that it was not up to me to intervene directly. I disregarded that objection, since I saw only too well that the time required to secure that service had the effect of keeping the child in an unresolved situation, perhaps for a long time.

As for the emergency situation to be considered, I gave notice that I could be called on weekends for a baby born confidentially, and that I would come in to speak to her. The idea was to intervene as soon as possible, based on the notion that there was the danger of a total break. In such cases, the child at birth is completely severed from all her prenatal perceptions; someone had to be there to name these perceptions, give them meaning, bridge the gap between the intrauterine past, the present, and the child's future.

This is a relative, or rather, a "preventive" emergency: its aim is more to prevent disaster than to remedy it; in matters of the psyche, the latter would be absurd and would only be an act of violence on the psychoanalyst's part. But it is an emergency. Of course, one must sometimes speak to a new-born who is sick, who is committing suicide or letting herself die, who wants to regress: These are speech emergencies in answer to the symptom. But in the case of confidential child-birth, the symptom is social; it is because we know it is so that we must act quickly. If no one intervenes, there is the risk that "true" symptoms, clinical this time, will surface.

This assurance that the matter is taken seriously has an effect on others besides the children and their mothers—on the staff in the first place. From what my colleagues report of experiences they have had in other places, where no one knew where to put these children or who ought to take care of them, the situation is healthier at Béclère. Here we know the things that can be done and the things that cannot. There is no longer any vagueness or uneasiness in the staff at the mere idea of taking care of a birth mother, since everyone knows it is an emergency and the psychoanalyst must be called in. This means there is less stress compromising the effectiveness of their work. That is true in both wards concerned (maternity and pediatrics), where I intervene specifically for confidential births, with the agreement of the senior consultant.

Similarly, when I tell babies about their lives, I do not forget to explain who is taking care of them and in what capacity: "So-and-so is taking care of you, she is there to console you when you are sad, to feed you. . . . That's what she's there for, that's her job. Someday you are going to have to separate from her, but there will always be other people like her to take care of you until an adoptive family has been found for you."

These simple and obvious words have the advantage of making the situation less alarming for the caregivers: Because they are said to be replaceable, they do not take themselves for substitute "mothers," with all the affective weight that can carry. In addition, I speak with them about what I am doing and why. I relieve them of what is not their responsibility so that they will help me fulfill my own, all for the newborn's benefit. That mutual reflection makes it possible to avoid placing the various teams in paradoxical situations.

At a time when no specific procedure existed, "nameless" children were placed in the kangaroo unit, the argument being that it was the only place where there would be time to coddle them. That was very much the case, in fact, and the members of the staff competed with one another even more than usual to give attentive care. These babies were brought all sorts of ribbons and bows to wear; they were set up in the latest car seat, surrounded by plush toys and embroidered outfits; everyone stopped to talk to them, passed the time with them; they were "their" babies. However, the anxiety did not drop proportionately. For it to be dissipated, we had to rethink the definition of the kangaroo unit, which is a *mother-child* unit: What were newborns given up by their parents doing in a unit designed to reinforce the connection between a mother and her child? It was therefore simply decided that "nameless" children would go to the neonatal unit if they needed intensive care, otherwise to pediatrics.

In the story of Pierrette, I said that it was obligatory for those seeking to give birth confidentially to meet with me. That was not always the case, and, here again, setting a procedure in place made that possible. In the past, I rarely saw pregnant women who were planning to give up their children, despite my desire to do so, because I had asked the social workers who saw them to suggest they see me at their convenience. The mothers often refused to meet with me, and, in the end, I understood that, nine times out of ten, the reason for that refusal rested on a misunderstanding: Apparently, they imagined I was going to ask them to explain themselves. When the two social workers with whom I had undertaken this venture left to put their talents to use elsewhere, I continued the same procedure with their successors.

I later gave myself permission to practice an obligatory consultation, feeling that, in an emergency situation, I was not a psychoanalyst in the strict sense, but a specialist with psychoanalytic training within the framework of a request made to the hospital—and not to me as a psychoanalyst. Hence, when a woman comes to the maternity ward for a confidential birth, she is now told: "If you want to give birth confidentially at Béclère Hospital, you must go see the social worker and then Dr. Szejer."

The conversation with the birth mother is an opportunity to listen and to work out a plan. It takes place under the terms of professional confidentiality, which exceeds medical confidentiality; that is, I do not retranscribe the content of the conversation in the medical file, with the exception of the patient's responses to legal specifications. My aim is to be sufficiently clear about what is to be transmitted to the child, especially if the mother does not want to see him, since I am the one in that case who will go talk to the child. It is best to get that compendium of information from the most authoritative source. There are often big surprises. Though I have sometimes prejudged a request for confidential childbirth that I felt was made without due consideration, there has not yet been a case where I have not changed my mind during the interview. The sincerity of these women, and the discovery they often make in the course of the discussion itself of the irrefutable reasons for their request, prevail over any other consideration.

I am not the only one to be surprised, nor the only one to change my mind. There was a young woman who, in the course of our conversation, told me of her desire to give birth confidentially. She did not want anything to do with her child; she explained to me that her boyfriend and she had been living together and had conceived the baby, but that she had found out that the boyfriend did not love her enough and had broken up with him. He did not know she was pregnant. She also did not want her family to know. The child, she said, would be better off in a real family than it would be with her, since she again found herself "in a jam," out of work. Hearing that, I blurted out: "But after all, you wanted that baby!"

I did not know exactly what I was saying, except that I understood they had conceived that child in full knowledge of the facts (they had not used contraception). When I saw her open her eyes wide and acquiesce as if, after all, that really was what she was thinking, I knew that my statement was on the order of an interpretation, an unveiling of an unconscious desire.

As such, it had its effect, and by the following meeting, she had decided to keep the child. She came back for that second conversation accompanied by one of her friends, in whom she had willingly confided, and to whom I had encouraged her to speak of our conversation. It is an understatement to say she was transformed: She was radiant, her belly prominent, and she said she felt like she was living a fairy tale. She had reestablished contact with her partner, having realized she was not obliged to share her life with him to give her child a father. From what she understood, he was not, strictly speaking, enthusiastic about the idea of the baby. We both told ourselves that the baby, when it arrived, might do what was required to ensnare him; otherwise, the baby would be strong enough to accommodate itself to its fate, since it would have been warned. Both would certainly be aided by the family, which, happy to welcome that new arrival, had promised its support.

This account of our conversation allows me, in passing, to dispel a few common misconceptions. The first is that, for some people, confidential childbirth functions as a palliative to abortion. I do not have the impression that this is the way things happen in reality; in any case, I have not observed it myself. This young woman would never have had an abortion under any terms, but she did not see how she could financially support that child. The second misconception is that, by explaining to the women who ask how adoption works, we are encouraging them to give the child up. This example proves the contrary.

Such a conversation also has an informative purpose. Together with the mothers, very conscientiously, we constitute a file. I tell them again the rights the law gives them, and I ask what they wish to transmit to the child and by what means: a letter, objects, words addressed directly to the child? We consider together what will be said, what will be left out, how and whether the father will be mentioned, all according to their wishes. In some hospital wards and nurseries, a little book illustrated with photos is added to the file, a book in which the nursing staff recounts the baby's first days. The pediatric team at Béclère makes up a little booklet containing simple phrases of extreme interest to these children: "You drank well today . . . yesterday, you cried all day . . . the psychoanalyst came to see you and told you your story, and since then you've been sleeping very well!" The booklets are for these children what the photo albums mothers put together with so much care are for other children. That indicates their importance. They are adoptees' most prized possession; since they have no mother to tell them of their first moments, this book is their only witness.

To support the mothers is one thing, to speak to the children is another, and it is just as key. The child has experienced a separation that does not yet make sense to him, and which is taboo for others. In one way or another, someone must tell him something about it: his mother; a psychoanalyst, if he happens to encounter one; or, at least, a person serving as a third party who allows words to be placed over the prenatal perceptions committed to memory. If these elements, which allow a newborn to get his bearings in the first moments of his life, are forever lost—odor, warmth, the mother's voice and the mother tongue, possibly the father's voice, the family atmosphere, but also the relating of "family stories"—they must be supplemented. Every person who feels able to speak to the child, who knows his history through the mother or who knows what the parents wanted to transmit to him, must make it her mission to intervene. Indeed, the only thing that establishes a connection are the words that will be pronounced for the child's benefit and which will give meaning to what is his lot in life. That person is, so to speak, a go-between, a messenger between the mother and child. She is the one who articulates, but not the one who consoles (the nursing staff is better able to do that). She can speak to the child because she does it at the mother's request. In the most problematic cases, when the mother has left no trace behind, one must also be able to speak to the child, if only to describe to him the circumstances of his birth.

I cannot insist enough on the fact that what may appear formal on my part is essential, because definitive separation is an ordeal for a newborn. French law has reduced the retraction period from three to two months. Had it reduced it to six weeks, that would still be too much for a newborn kept in a state of weightlessness, in an undefined symbolic space. For a human being to be able to consider itself human, the cut I spoke of regarding the baby blues must be made. For a child born confidentially, an external word must bring about that cut, thereby constituting the sort of psychic groundwork necessary for its development. That word should never be sequestered later on, as we will see is sometimes the case; the child must be able to grow up without stumbling into the holes of the secret. He will then be able to take his place in that very particular history that precedes and permeates him.

All the principles of that procedure are simple. Their merit, in my opinion, is to inform future mothers, who often are not informed, so that they can decide with full knowledge of the facts. To listen, to work with the mother, to prepare for the child's relinquishment if the decision has been made, to

work it out, to speak to the child: All that allows us to mini-
mize the discomfort created by the applicable laws, and to
apply them while respecting the children and their parents.
That amounts to relieving the weight on the future child's
shoulders, and, for the staff, it is an assurance that things are
said and that it is not necessary to "remedy" an unfortunate
fate through irresponsible and impulsive acts. After all, a
confidential birth is not a misfortune, and it takes a minimum level of serenity to respect it.

THE PAIN OF CONFIDENTIAL CHILDBIRTH

As one can imagine, confidential childbirth very often follows a social tragedy: rape, incest, material or emotional destitution, psychological or even physical pressure from friends
and family. The list of circumstances surrounding confidential birth is painfully consistent.

In certain countries, children die because they were
"unplanned" (conceived outside marriage, in adultery, etc.).
They do not receive the care they ought to have at birth. The
pressures are such that the mothers risk their lives as well.
They are placed in a position of believing that, for them, it is
better to be dead than to dishonor the family.

A few years ago, women from these countries came to
give birth confidentially in France. Confidential childbirth
as it is stipulated by law exists only in France, Luxembourg,
and Italy. They came, they said, because they as well as their
children felt threatened by family vengeance; they were not
forgiven for their "illegitimate" pregnancy. They spoke of being locked away, abducted, of their babies being left to die. In
some sense, they were demanding political asylum for their

unborn child, and for that reason asked to give birth anonymously. We see practically no cases of that kind today. The French policy restricting visas closed the door to that refuge. Who is the better for it: these women, their children, or immigration services?

We now see women living in Muslim fundamentalist enclaves in Paris who conceal their pregnancies, give birth confidentially, and rejoin their families as if nothing had happened. They live as de facto illegal immigrants even if they are not so by law, and feel there is no possibility for them to bring up a child. Nearly any choice other than confidential birth is barred them. If they agreed to leave their community of origin and accept the social workers the state assigns to them in order to keep their child, they would put their own life or that of their baby in danger. They would be pariahs.

When there is no social tragedy, a psychological tragedy is almost always at issue in a confidential childbirth. As far as tragic circumstances are concerned, the Third World or populations living under extreme conditions (destitution, war) have no monopoly: All social classes are represented in the area of confidential births.

Fortunately, there are counterexamples to these tragedies, and on certain occasions it is even possible to speak of confidential childbirth by mutual agreement. Let me mention the example of a forty-five-year-old woman admitted to the hospital emergency room for acute abdominal pains. The intern examined her, then, suspecting it was a fibroid, sent her to be evaluated by maternity emergency, where it was discovered that she was quite simply in labor. She thus learned she was pregnant as she was giving birth. I was present on the ward while she was in the labor room and was asked to go see her because she was in quite a state, as one can well imagine. Unfortunately, the doctors and midwives, though aware of the harshness of the situation she was going through, had to deal with other emergencies, and it therefore fell to me to support her.

She confided to me that she already had three children and that this birth was occurring at a time when the couple was having problems. She maintained that, because she was so unhappy with her husband, her first three children were not thriving, and she did not wish to add to the fourth's unhappiness. She said her husband was an alcoholic, violent and abusive toward her, and that was already enough. The situation was terrible for her, and, as one can imagine, she spoke poignantly of her dilemma: She acknowledged her child and, at the same time, thought she could not take responsibility for him, fearing she would impose her own misfortune on him. The solution that seemed best to her was "for him to be able to grow up in a thriving family with a happy mother capable of transmitting happiness." She thus gave birth confidentially and gave up the child for adoption. In the file we assembled together, she left a letter with her address and phone number, with the wish he could obtain them whenever he wanted. The father was informed, and also agreed to this.

Most of the time, however, requests for confidential childbirth are not automatic, and those making the requests are not always aware it is legally possible. These requests arise during a medical visit in the course of the pregnancy or just after delivery. We therefore have a mission to inform and explain, to allow these women to make a choice.

Once the decision to give birth confidentially has been

made, all the women I have seen are deeply moved, even those who did not want to keep the child, even those who felt that the possibility granted by the law was a gift to the child.

Some will end up changing their minds during the two-month period they are given. This is rare, and, truth be told, in most cases, the about-face has unhappy consequences. Very often, in fact, once they have decided to reclaim their parental rights, they do not come to see the baby, or come very rarely. The result is probably the worst one imaginable for the child: She is given up de facto if not de jure, but cannot be adopted so long as her parents show up, even occasionally. Trapped in that situation, she will be raised in an institution. In other cases, the mothers take back their children but mistreat them. That mistreatment, in almost all cases, is a repetition of the brutality they themselves endured.

Some waver for a long time without making a clear decision. Once I assisted a woman, whom I asked, as I customarily do, if she wanted us to go together to speak to her child or if she preferred that I go by myself. She asked that I accompany her and, when she saw him, declared: "I'm not abandoning you!" You can imagine my perplexity, since the term "abandon," even eliminated from the wording of the law, can be used, as here, in all its ambiguity: What does it mean to declare one is abandoning a child and then say: "I'm not abandoning you"? Did she or did she not want to place her child for adoption? Did she mean she had changed her mind or simply that she would keep her child in her thoughts? In fact, it was the latter. But that makes no allowances for her ambivalence, which lasted until the end of the period granted her by law.

I heard more about that waffling subsequently. It seems

that, after the child's birth, he was rehospitalized in the pediatric ward for respiratory problems. I saw him again at that time, and offered him an interpretation that had good results. I suggested he was trying, through his troubles, to reestablish an umbilical—that is, "prerespiratory"—mode of communication.

"It is as if, in coming back to the hospital, you were looking for your mother where she left you. But she's gone, and she has not changed her mind: She placed you in the nursery until a family is found to adopt you. What you can find again, as much as you like, what you will never lose, is her memory: You can always keep it inside you."

The difficulties ended and he was able to return to the nursery. Shortly thereafter, the mother returned to the hospital to reclaim her child, and she was told he was at the nursery. She waited more than three months after the birth—to be precise, exactly one day after the expiration of the fateful grace period—to ask to retrieve the child. Part of her wanted to give him up, the other refused, but the second side was weaker and she managed to arrive too late and to allow the first side to win out.

The nursery staff, seeing the child caught on the seesaw of his mother's contradictory desires, decided to send him to one of their psychoanalyst consultants. They wanted to know if the child was psychologically ready to be adopted. From what I was told, it appears he was.

Family Secrets, State Secrets

Regarding confidential births, we use the term *confidential,* that is, *secret,* a word that takes into account matters beyond our immediate comprehension. In Latin, what is *secretus* is "separated," "broken up" (from *secernere,* to separate, to sort). According to the same etymology, something that is a *secretio* is "set apart." The issue in these births is to "secrete secrecy," to *set apart* something concerning the *separation* involved in these particular births, and what is set apart often has to do with the baby's conception. There is a likelihood that, for the adopted child and for following generations, this secret will become a *family secret.* In that respect, the child born confidentially will not escape a fate common to all the world's children.

FAMILY SECRETS AND FAMILY ROMANCES

Let us leave aside for a moment the restricted field of confidential childbirth and interest ourselves in these family secrets that are everyone's fate. What are family secrets? Neither more nor less than what feeds all family romances, and hence the Oedipus complex. Moreover, these secrets need not be known to operate; they need only exist. It is they that can resurface in the baby blues for example, at the moment after birth, which produces the opening to the unconscious discussed earlier. That is often an opportunity to articulate family secrets, "illegitimate" conceptions, and other "skeletons in the closet." Grandparents and visiting aunts loosen their tongues when a child is born.

The newborn, whether or not she was affected by that secret during her prenatal life, can then benefit from that revelation. We must make an effort to see that it is made in front of her, must help the parents to speak, to say things they would not have said elsewhere, sometimes even to realize the importance of these secrets they were keeping buried. Thereby, we can hope to ensure that the child, in addition to the more or less difficult circumstances of her conception and birth, does not have to bear the weight of guilt connected to the secret.

Family secrets can weigh on the newborn, and even on the fetus. Catherine Dolto, in a meeting of the organization La Cause des Bébés (The Interests of the Child), said that if, during a haptonomy session, the couple revealed a family secret, she felt the fetus react. Perhaps it shared the secret? Just as we have been able to speak of prenatal sensoriality, I think the child knows something about it, but does not know what. When Catherine Dolto says that revealing family secrets affects the fetus via the pregnant woman, we must understand that the fetus is committing perceptions to memory, which it may or may not be able to connect to words after its birth.

The characteristic of these family secrets is to transmit the unexpressed, an empty space that crosses generations. It is not only the fetus or newborn who is affected, but the individual over the course of a lifetime, and even his or her descendants.

SECRETS AND ANONYMITY: THE PERSPECTIVE OF THE LAW AND THE PSYCHOANALYST

Family secrets travel across generations. The unexpressed in a family history creates a gulf, as it were, that calls upon subjects to find their bearings. These family secrets are, we might say, lacking in their pure state, a hole in the weave that cannot be mended. That gap is constitutive of all families; none escapes it. Nevertheless, not everyone goes crazy because of it, since we always have an imaginative recourse, however deformed it may be, to the histories of our ancestors, the origins of our family lines. If we rethink confidential childbirth from that perspective, we see that, in such cases, imaginative recourse can be rendered very difficult if the person knows nothing about his ancestors.

French law spreads even more confusion, if that is possible. It considers "nonidentifying" elements transmissible and not subject to confidentiality: the mother's weight, height, the color of her eyes and skin, and so on. Beyond that, it reserves the right to prohibit the transmission of the very things that make sense of a life. Beyond preserving the mother's anonymity, it runs the risk of denying her child the right to his origins.

Through the right to anonymity it grants mothers, French law allows our country to pursue its vocation as a land of refuge: It saves human lives, those of the women in danger I mentioned earlier, for example. But, in selecting among the nonidentifying elements those it judges appropriate, it prohibits adoptees, in the absence of an origin, from gaining permanent and unconditional access to their histories. The child is in quest of the narrative that will allow him to answer the question: Why did they give me up? To know that answer is as necessary to the foundations of his existence as to know who gave him up. It is in being able to answer those two questions that he too will more easily be able to adopt a family, its history, and the identity it offers him.

In practice, the law obliges him to conform to the order to ignore what, *unconsciously,* he knows. What will happen to that child after birth? Without attachments, tossed willy-nilly by everyone's projected parental fantasies, he will often be entrusted to the guardianship of the police prefect and the custody of the county, which, through the intermediary of Children's Services and Family Counseling, assumes responsibility for him until adoption. These guardian institutions claim for themselves the right to select from his history what it is appropriate and inappropriate to transmit "in the interest of the child." In so doing, they give themselves permission to censor certain information provided by the mother, which they judge without relevance for him. This information is censored supposedly in the interest of the child, but it is very often the interest or reputation of the adoptive parents that is at issue. How, then, could the adoptive parents fail to yield to the temptation to efface that unfortunate preadoption history? And, even if they did resist, how could the child find his bearings? Through that censorship masking as pedagogy or morality, these institutions idealize a certain view of motherhood and parenthood. Such a view cannot serve the child, as far as I'm concerned, since, let us admit it: It creates indisputable collective ties of silence. These secrets for the benefit of society create speech orphans and manufacture "too" adoptable children, children outside family lines, the children of everyone and of no one.

Very often, women who are thinking about giving birth confidentially create a family secret regarding the conception, especially if it involved rape or incest. They want nothing of all that to be transmitted to the child. Sometimes, they even want nothing to be transmitted about the biological father. One has to respect these requests, because they come from the mother. But one must specify in the file: "For her own reasons, Mrs. X does not wish to speak of the biological father, nor of the conditions of this child's conception, inasmuch as she considers it her private life." A simple sentence like that can change everything, because the biological father has been designated as existing; there is no exclusion.

The situation is entirely different when a social worker, because she knows, writes on the file, "rape or incest," and a state agency, upon reading that information, censors it. That is sheer madness, and serves to make the *family secret* a *state secret*. It is as if the state agency, as stipulated by law, took itself for the family. On the contrary, that service ought to confirm the information and transmit it in full to the adoptive family. If the adoptive family temporarily censors some elements for pedagogical reasons, it will all the same be in a position to raise the child in terms of what he is.

An adoptive family that has knowledge of a family secret communicated by the birth mother can deal with it by telling the child: "We don't know anything, because your birth mother did not want us to know anything." This differs radically from state censorship, since, in this case, the future is preserved.

Let us take the case of women from the former Yugoslavia. We are familiar with the policy of systematic rape within the context of ethnic cleansing, just as we learned of the Third Reich's eugenics experiments. Some Bosnian women were able to give birth confidentially in France. As a result, from the inexpressible pain affecting them, this country helped to give life to something human, a living response to the barbarism that had engendered it. Let us now suppose that a family adopts a Bosnian child, knowing her origins. To say nothing to the child, even with the intention of not damaging her, would be asking her, in some sense, to conform to the model of a child she is not. She too has a memory, an unconscious one in any case, and we should not be too surprised if she does not feel very comfortable in that costume concocted for her, since it does not belong to her. It is not adoption in itself that can cause difficulties for these children, but rather the way in which it is negotiated.

Sometimes adopted children later display a symptom associated with the secrets that weigh upon them. At least they will then be allowed to try to penetrate these secrets, to make investigations as far as they can, as they wish. In itself, getting to the bottom of a secret does not necessarily liberate the subject from a potential symptom (though this has often been seen), but at least using it as she understands it will. It is therefore always up to the families—adoptive or biological— to oversee the fate of that secret; it is surely not up to a state or adoption agency. The families are free to hold back one thing or another as a function of what they judge appropriate for the child to know at one age or another. It will then be a temporary secret, reflecting a pedagogical concern on their part, and no longer a definitive erasure of part of what makes the child a living being. Adoption agencies in France now agree that families are to be advised to raise their child with her truth. We must hope, in addition, that that truth has not been adulterated further up the line.

Must the secret of the parents' origins and anonymity be guaranteed? French law tends to impose the secret of origins; enlightened specialists call solely for anonymity. For my part, I propose a compromise solution in the application of the law. As a psychoanalyst, I start from the principle that all formulable discourse contains missing statements. The situation of a child resulting from a confidential birth is no exception. Nevertheless, no one must claim the right, as part of her practice, to represent the lack that inhabits the unconscious, to make a selection. I simply ask society, that is, the institutions that form its framework, to respect that rule, and to not manipulate the nonidentifying elements at will. In point of fact, reality is contradictory, and every problem has its solution. Children's Services in France offers the guarantee of a hermetic secret. It is a reliable and responsible institution, which knows how to ensure to anyone who asks that nothing or almost nothing will be said. That is the best assurance for the woman who displays a desire for a total break, for example, by not seeing her child at birth, by not leaving a letter or object for him, or by asking that everything about the father be left unsaid. In the case of a woman who wishes to receive news of the adopted child, or who hopes that a letter or objects they have left for him will be transmitted, certain private adoption agencies are often better situated for this. They tend to be more open. [2]

There are cases where even more openness and generosity exist. In French Polynesia, for example, there is something very close to a tradition of "child giving." Adoption operates through a transfer of parental authority over the course of two years. For two years (and two months, since the retraction period is added), the child lives with her adoptive parents. After that period, if the agreement between the biological and adoptive parents has endured, the adoption is pronounced final. Sometimes residents of metropolitan France go to seek a child in Tahiti, get to know the family of origin, and are delegated parental authority. When they return to the metropolis with the child, they remain in contact with the family of origin through letters, videocassettes, and photos. When the adoption is final, everything, in the best of all possible worlds, usually works out, and there is gratitude on both sides. An unexpected but logical consequence of this system is that contraception is rarely practiced there, since, if you have an extra baby, you give it away.

Today in France, the law displays its value as well as its limitations. Its value lies in pushing society toward a better symbolic and ethical recognition of the members that constitute it, even if that law reflects the views of only a minority.

An example? By virtue of the adoption law passed in 1996, society recognizes that it is intolerable for individuals to exist in its bosom without a name: It prefers "Sandra" to "Exette," to allude to the case already mentioned. All the same, it does not guarantee a child the right to his history, does not recognize the positive aspect of the action of a mother who gives birth confidentially; it acts as if it preferred to defend a remnant of puerile and polite civility. It is as if the law had to give credence to those who see confidential childbirth as an obvious or hidden shame, and who might say: "That mother's action or intention is shady, better keep it quiet for good," or "Mr. or Mrs. X abandoned their child; as a result, they are on the fringes of the social order. For the rest, let's not ask ourselves any questions, since the formalities of love are being respected."

Nevertheless, to be respectful (and desirous) of the law does not mean one is enamored of tidiness. A psychoanalyst, for her part, may be placed in the position of maintaining that a woman who gives (up) her child is performing an act of love and that, conversely, a woman who force-feeds her child is not necessarily performing one. In other words, although the law's intention is good, its interpretation leaves room for confusion if we are not careful. Only adequate training of the nursing staff faced with these problems can help ensure that the law is applied in the interests of the child, the mother, and the father.

SAMIA DOES NOT FEEL STRONG ENOUGH

When society offers women low-cost single-parent housing, cash allocations, or some other aid, its intention is good. But does it realize it is simultaneously canceling out what it offers by demanding in turn a renunciation from the mother: to break off with her father, her mother, her brothers and sisters, the lover who has dropped out of sight, tradition, culture, holidays? What sort of place, future, or ideal does it give her to be a mother and raise her child? Samia found herself in such a dilemma. She was an Arab, and discovered she was pregnant by a Frenchman she had known for a long time and with whom she was living. They had done nothing to prevent conception, and probably even hoped for it.

Neither of the two families approved of the union. His family leaned toward the views of the National Front, an extremely right wing and racist political group; hers had a somewhat Islamist view of things. These families barely tolerated the couple, and did not fail to pile on racial slurs directed at "the other side" whenever the occasion presented itself.

In Samia's fourth month of pregnancy, when she was beginning to show, the child's father suddenly declared he no longer wanted it. Not managing to convince (himself) with words, he began to hit Samia. She reached the point of fearing not only for herself, but also for her baby. She thus left home and sought refuge with a relative. A few months later, having reached her delivery date, she came to give birth at Béclère, and expressed her wish to give up the child.

Why was this man, against all expectations given his past behavior, capable of reacting so violently? I hypothesized that, confronted with his own father's racism, he no longer felt strong enough to be the father of a child conceived with an Arab woman, as soon as that pregnancy became evident to everyone, including his father. She, hearing her family say it was because she had chosen a Frenchman that she found herself in that disastrous situation, felt too weak to combat these two forces of intolerance. Both were lacking in strength. Financially, their situation was adequate to welcome that child, whom they had wanted, but they would have had to break away from their own families, and that was too much for them. Who could reproach them? Not I, in any case, since I know from experience that most people who give up a child have no strength left.

I therefore worked with Samia in her decision to give birth confidentially without seeing the child. She wished thereby to avoid the break with her family and her partner's violence toward her or toward their child. She named her child and asked me to tell him their entire story. She then composed a letter, leaving her address and phone number, so that he could find her if he wished, following the legal formalities we indicated to her. She finally asked that he be entrusted to a private adoption agency, intent that the letter be transmitted as is, without censorship.

Before talking with Samia, I was in a mood that lent itself

to every sort of serious error. Knowing nothing but her file, I had come to wonder why she was there, and why she had not gotten prenatal care from the beginning. None of the reasons given seemed to me to explain her request, and I was almost ready to treat her to a little tirade about decency, arguing that you do not give up a child simply because you don't feel like having one. Was this a young woman who not only did not "feel" like a mother but did not want to risk becoming one at any cost? Of course, there is no maternal instinct, as French philosopher Elisabeth Badinter has emphasized. But I was to the point of interpreting her request without hearing it, re-membering similar past cases. Was there, on her part, a form of violence that consists of not giving a child the chance to make you a mother because you cannot bear renouncing your own mother or your status as a child? I was indulging in presuppositions that could lead me only to the dysfunction I denounced earlier in some members of the nursing staff.

That day, I was still affected by another, very young mother I had seen shortly before, and who had shaken my convictions. She too had absolutely nothing "against" the child. She had succeeded in hiding her pregnancy from her family—it is astonishing to see how a woman who wants to deny or conceal her pregnancy can succeed in her aims. And then, late at night, without waking anyone, she gave birth to her child and deposited it in the trash room. I said "de-posited": I ought to have said "displayed." She did not get rid of the child as one might think, but wrapped it in a terry towel and laid it out in the trash room of her apartment building. Finally, she went on her way to school. Police officers found the baby and soon identified the mother, whom they immediately placed under close watch at the hospital. It was there that we met. Driven by the same prejudices, I asked the question: "What did you think would happen to the child in that garbage can?"

She responded very logically that she knew the garbage was about to be collected and that, therefore, he would be found quickly; then, come what may, she couldn't change anything. There was no trace in her words of any disregard for the child's life; it was more simply an incapacity to think of herself as the mother of that baby.

In her case, as in Pierrette's, the conversation, simply by virtue of obliging me to listen to her, led me to change my position radically. It once more placed me in the role of a psychoanalyst. Without these conversations, the harsh application of the law would have had no meaning, for her or for me.

From my position as a psychoanalyst, I am obliged to verify the veracity of the adage: The law is harsh but it is the law. The law exists, so much the better; it lends itself to confusion, so much the worse. But, beyond the files and statements the law prescribes, it is up to us as psychoanalysts, caregivers, and representatives of guardian institutions to oversee its modes of application in a way to guarantee to newborns that not too many pages are missing from the text of their lives.

Being Born Is Not Everything

The baby blues and confidential childbirth have been considered in separate chapters, but as issues they are intimately related. The first places the mother with her child center stage, whereas the second separates them. In one case, a connection is difficult to maintain; in the other, a connection is difficult to sever. Why make them into a single object of interest for the psychoanalyst?

It is because both mark the decisive step leading from birth to humanization and characterize the difficulty of that period of limbo. To speak of limbo is to speak of an edge or threshold. The child is on the edge of completing her birth in the eyes of those who have welcomed her. What is the nature of that edge, of that suspension between the real and the symbolic? Is it, for the child, a time of anxious waiting, of hope, or is it a delay without rhyme or reason? Etymology provides an optimistic version: In fourteenth-century ecclesiastical Latin, limbo *(limbi)* is "the heavenly abode located on the edge of paradise." It is the place where the souls of the just who died before the coming of Christ await their deliverance. That usage branches off to designate the abode of the souls of children who died without being baptized into the Catholic religion.

Children born confidentially may be closer to hell than to paradise. Someone must speak to them to allow them to get out of limbo. Some psychiatrists have made a connection between these abandoned children and people who commit suicide. Both are felt to be unseemly and guilt-inducing; they are disturbing and have around them an odor of sin. As the historian Yvonne Knibiehler reminds us, legal procedures for giving up a child have always sought to give the "fallen woman" a means to efface her "sin." It was believed she "could not feel any affection for her child, an object of shame, and the child itself would feel only disdain and resentment toward the one who inflicted such a life on it. The *unwed* could not be *mothers*. . . . What historical knowledge establishes is precisely that the desire for a child among women was never freely expressed.... The problem is that of the child's *humanization,* her insertion and functionality in the service of *civilized* human societies."[3]

Children born confidentially and children caught within their mothers' baby blues must all get out of limbo in order to be born to the symbolic. Could it be that birth is not such a natural thing?

Born to Society

In the maternity ward, everything begins with birth. This is a truism, hardly contradicted by the prenatal care for high-risk pregnancies and the medically assisted reproductive services provided at the same hospital. The foremost aim is still birth. It is said it is the first natural act of life.

From a medical point of view, there is nothing that permits us to be satisfied with such an assertion. The experience of doctors in a maternity hospital is riddled with unexplained facts, births that "fall short" for no reason, unexpected deaths in utero, prophylactic treatments that inexplicably fail, unpreventable sudden deaths. Should we simply not interfere with the natural course of events and attribute everything to fate? For the obstetrician, this is not possible. Understanding is the foundation of his research, his education, his power, and his passion.

For the anthropologist, birth, before being a simple biological fact, is a matter of culture. Let us recall the assertions of Françoise Héritier, who argues that there is seemingly no society that confuses filiation and generation.[4] As a Samo proverb that inspired her says: "It is the word that produces filiation, it is the word that takes it away." If the child is not named by the community he enters through his birth, he is not merely banished from society; quite simply, he does not exist.

For members of ethics committees and all those who have recently had to debate new reproductive technologies, confidential childbirth, and adoption, birth is also an eminently social problem, beginning with its mere possibility. Who will say, for example, that every person or infertile couple has the right to a child, on the pretext that the new technologies can procure it for them? Can one appeal to the right of a child (not yet in existence) to be born in order to apply these technologies under any conditions whatsoever? How must the law choose, arbitrate, and, in the end, determine who is the father of a child when the biological father, presumed dead, reappears once the mother has remarried after completing her "mourning"? What about a surrogate mother who demands the right to educate a child with the argument that a contract was signed to that effect with the parents (in the United States, for example, since the law prohibits that practice in France)? Whatever the body of law, substantial in this matter, the problem is constant: Who is the son or daughter of whom? By virtue of what intervention by society will a law of kinship decide on a newborn's existence?

FROM BIRTH TO ACKNOWLEDGMENT

Lawmakers have decided. For them, birth is followed by acknowledgment. The parents declare the birth, the public records official at city hall records it—or, as in certain large maternity hospitals, his delegate does so at the hospital: "Born today, Jean/Jeanne, son/daughter of Maurice Gendron and Julie, his wife, born Jarniguet; which we, as officers of the court, have recorded this day, etc." If the parents do not declare the birth, someone else must: a civil servant at city hall, in the case of a foundling or when no name was given by the parents; the midwife, in the case of a confidential childbirth. The declaration of acknowledgment follows. It is granted automatically when the parents are married; otherwise, it requires the mother and possibly the father to go to city hall. In cases where one or the other does not acknowledge the child or retracts that acknowledgment, the situation becomes a little more complicated. For example, there is a stipulation in French law for "acknowledgment before birth"; for unmarried couples, the mother can acknowledge the child before it is born and it will then bear her last name. After birth, the father may also acknowledge the child; in that case, both last names will be used. Society's intervention at birth occurs in other ways as well. Even though its power is rarely exercised in our time, the public records office or, at its request, the district attorney, can reject a name "in the interest of the child." It can even call for an inquiry into biological kinship, etc. Public birth records have existed for barely two centuries, and the baptismal registries that preceded them were notoriously incomplete. In short, society's statistical preoccupation is a modern imperative. Nevertheless, people were born before it took hold. The social intervention, however, is not without consequences, sometimes even absurd ones, for the newborn. Hence, so long as the three days French law grants to declare the birth has not elapsed, the newborn has no legal existence. During her stay in the maternity ward, she quite simply does not exist, except in the eyes of her family and caregivers. The only way the child can get out of that situation of being alive while having no existence is to be hospitalized in another ward for special care, in pediatrics, for example; only at that moment will she be declared under her name. Until then, only the mother who entered the maternity ward is acknowledged by the hospital administration.

NAMING

Birth is the appearance of a being conceived by two other human beings, a being who has lost its exclusive physiological dependence on the one who carried it in her womb, and who is recognized as a member of the human community. At issue, therefore, is the act of naming. That is not self-evident, or rather, it does not go without *saying*. Whether it's the wild child or Kaspar Hauser, a child has to be acknowledged by his peers to recognize he is alive. For the psychoanalyst, what is at issue is language and the body, *speech tethered to the body*: a newborn who is not inscribed in one way or another by the human beings who are supposed to welcome him is, in a certain way, little different from a UFO. To the question raised regarding the child's status between the time he is delivered and the declaration of his birth, a psychoanalyst replies that she knows he is alive by the desires that led him to that point; but that she also knows that the nonacknowledgment of his desire can mean, at the least, symbolic death. Of course, naming is not, in this case, a simple problem of legal declaration or even the attribution of a given name. It also involves the indispensable utterance of the child's history. The child must *hear spoken* a minimum of his history and his inscription within the parental lineage (that is, that of his father and mother, but also that of their forebears if possible). It is here that, if the parents cannot do it, a third party can intervene. Otherwise, the unthought can produce a symptom.

Birth is neither a natural act nor a mere story. It is perhaps more difficult to conceive of than death, because it is not inevitable. We have seen that certain babies were able to choose to die before birth. We are like the character in Umberto Eco's novel who "took to dreaming about his birth, of which he knew even less than about his death. It is said that thinking about origins is what characterizes the philosopher. It is easy for the philosopher to justify death: the idea that one ought to rush headlong into darkness is one of the clearest things in the world. What haunts the philosopher is not the naturalness of the end, but the mystery of the beginning. We may lose interest in the eternity that will follow us, but we cannot remove ourselves from the agonizing enigma of the eternity that preceded us."[5]

As everyone knows, the condition for life is death, and the condition for living well is the foreknowledge of death.

As a result, getting out of limbo depends on the response to the question: Are we here to live happily, as much as we can? What is played out in the first three or four days of life, in short, can be articulated in simple terms: "Being born is not everything, one has to live after all!" The chorus of newborns quickly echoes: "That's all we're asking!"

Nevertheless, it seems there are a few sour notes in the chorus, since certain babies behave as if that were not at all obvious.

Epilogue: The Choice to Live

"The word is man, his memory, and his future." —EDMOND
JABÈS

In hospitals and public institutions, psychoanalysis is no longer as welcome as it was in the 1970s; it is asked to be discreet. There is no longer a collaboration between psychiatry and psychoanalysis, as there once was. Official psychiatry no longer sees psychoanalysis as a reference point. As a result, little room is left for the specificity of the psychic symptom. We need to move beyond the debate between psychiatry and psychoanalysis, which is unproductive in many ways. Everyone can at least agree on one point, namely, that beyond their respective positions and ethics, psychiatrists and psychoanalysts have a social obligation toward those who consult them.

The modernity of psychoanalysis lies in seeing that this obligation is not imposed violently on clients; that is, its aim is to recognize the truth of every human being before reducing him to his symptom. That ethical imperative summons psychoanalysis to return to action through the discovery of new fields, new practices, and a new effectiveness.

In the area of perinatality with which I am concerned, one of the new fields is the period of limbo; by their essence, the baby blues, on which I have focused, escape standard psychiatric treatment. They are not listed as a specific pathology, and are not "treated" as such when they appear. Conversely, the psychoanalyst, who chooses to see them as a first moment in the constitution of the subject, will be careful to listen to them attentively. Later on, she will have to enter areas left fallow by existing therapies, but on which the life of human beings is constructed: postnatal care for new mothers, the support of infants and parents in difficulty, but also procedures to help with childbirth and a consideration of prenatal life. In all these areas, there are many things to say and to discover from a psychoanalytic point of view.

At the level of practice, the first innovation required of the psychoanalyst may be that she leave her office and go to the patient: in the maternity ward, in the hospital, anywhere listening may allow her to modify the course of pathologies. That would presuppose establishing precise protocols inspired by psychoanalysis, regarding prevention or the general treatment of requests. That has been at issue for confidential childbirth, prevention directed at premature infants or at newborns whose history was marked by prior grief, and, more generally, for the identification and treatment of requests by parents and/or children. The result would be to bear witness, allowing trainees to acquire expertise through that experience. The most urgent and pressing need is to rethink the transposition of the psychoanalytic context to an institutional practice. The request evolves constantly, and in a direction that, in this time of social crisis, makes listening difficult. Psychoanalysts must adapt, must find an outcome to that request. In striving to do so, they keep intact their capacity for a human response to it. At a time when some protest that, amid the surge in social tragedies, we must attend to the most urgent cases, psychoanalysts, in many cases, can still consider listening to pain their first priority. At the level of effectiveness, which, like every social project, is measured over time, what we need in the first place are new capacities for operation. When the baby blues are not taken into consideration by psychiatrists in the three or four days after birth, depression sometimes follows and persists. This depression, which might have been prevented, is a common reason for office visits. The more time elapses between the baby blues and the treatment, the longer that treatment will take. Is it not more "economical" to be present earlier, before we have a syndrome to deal with? Remember, this is the same argument that motivated me in the case of confidential childbirth. But it may also apply to people of different ages and to other problematic situations. It only verifies one of the constants of our profession: The effect of interpretation is measured less by its pertinence than by its capacity to intervene in a timely manner. Interpretation follows the same logic as bearing witness, which, as I said in the introduction, has served as a guide for this book. Interpretation is a matter of scansion (scanning the speech of the analysand), and the new approach to newborns may lead to the first moment, the moment when one must decide on an action: "After the time for understanding the moment to conclude comes the moment to conclude the time for understanding."[1]

In emphasizing the period of limbo, I have done nothing more than attempt to reduce the psychic, social, and financial cost of the child's early difficulties. That preventive role, filled in this case by the psychoanalyst, is well received by the Béclère staff, even though it may seem alien to the needs of their practice. It may prove useful in many other places.

Children's Services in France, which sends some infants to the psychoanalyst's office under the rubric "nonreimbursable care," has the courage thereby to show that the cost of psychoanalysis is not undue or excessive in relation to what it offers. In so doing, as the responsible guardian it is for these children, it sanctions the therapeutic function of listening psychoanalytically to young children as prevention, as well as in the treatment of symptoms.

Many of the parents who consult psychoanalysts believe in that preventive function as well. When, after a few sessions, they have been able to find in themselves the resources to speak to their newborn, even in the midst of the profound suffering assailing them, they are pleased to spare him the troubles that, until that time, had ruined everyone's life: their baby's life, and even those of family and friends.

The complexity of the symptoms, especially in the child and newborn, often makes the diagnosis difficult. Sometimes these children seem to require psychotherapy when, in reality, they suffer from an organic ailment. Even more often, what manifests itself as a physiological disorder with an unclear course of treatment is shown, through psychoanalysis, to have psychic causes.

A three-year-old child was sent to me by his pediatrician, who was concerned because he slept very poorly and his insomnia was resistant to every treatment. He had been treated to every possible and imaginable exploratory procedure. Nothing worked, no diagnosis had been made, and the child was still an insomniac. All he had gained was a firm revulsion

for medical treatment and hospitals, which verged on a pho-
bia. After a month of visits to my office, the symptom, as
sometimes happens, disappeared.

What are we to think of the number of chronic ear infections and nose and throat inflammations that diminish when
the children who suffer from them undergo psychotherapy?
Why do these children, who have spent years swallowing
antibiotics, give up their symptoms after a few months of
therapy? This phenomenon has been clinically noted. Conclusions may be drawn, or not, about the relation between
the disappearance of the symptom and the therapy; that is a
question of professional conscience. But how can that relation be denied?

Similarly, I have had the opportunity to see certain resistant cases of asthma disappear during psychoanalytic treatment. That was the case for a little seven-year-old boy. His
life and his family's life was governed by the water cures prescribed him for every school vacation. He consulted a highly
renowned allergist who, tired of a symptom that resisted his
treatments, finally blurted out to the parents, who had asked
for his opinion about the advisability of psychoanalytic treatment: "If you have time and money to waste, then, by all
means, send your son!"

The child wasted a few months, perhaps a year, bringing
up all the family problems haunting him. Until then, his parents had sought to protect him from them, and did not suspect the suffocating situation in which they had placed their
son. In any case, having lost all that time with consistency
and application, the little patient lost his asthma as well.

Although the psychoanalyst insists on the therapeutic
powers of her approach, she must refuse to encroach on a ter-

ritory that is not her own. Just as she must not take herself for a midwife when she works in the maternity ward, not even a midwife of words, she must not act as a physician. Otherwise, she runs the risk of no longer being a psychoanalyst. If she is both a psychiatrist and a psychoanalyst, she will have to choose between her two roles. In the maternity ward, either I prescribe medication and offer the address of a psychoanalyst colleague, whom the patient will decide to see or not, or I fulfill my duties as a psychoanalyst and refrain from prescribing. The therapeutic effect of psychoanalytic listening comes at that price. Conversely, a doctor will be all the more effective if she does not play the "shrink." Her clinical instincts, that is, her technical understanding and sense of the human, can help her get her patient to request psychotherapeutic assistance, but it is not within the doctor's field of competence. Very often, a "shrink" intimidates people who have never seen one, and it would be too cruel to explain to the patient that his illness is more psychological than physiological and that he must consult a specialist. But to help the patient move beyond his fear to the point of handing over the reins to the psychoanalyst is already therapeutic: It humanizes suffering rather than technicizing it. Practitioners of the body can benefit from considering recourse to a specialist of the psyche not as a failure imputable to them, but as hope for a synergy to everyone's advantage.

In speaking of the crucial three- or four-day period following birth, I pretended to ignore the strange correspondence it has with the three or four days following conception. In prenatal life, the fourth day is when the egg migrates to the uterus and life begins; in postnatal life, it is the time of a symbolic birth. Could this be a variant of Dolto's "organic clock"?

Metaphorically in any case, it evokes to perfection the dimension of speech and symbolic coding that interests psychoanalysis. The real exists, but it can be apprehended only through its connection with the imaginary and the symbolic weaving it allows every individual. I hope I have shown this through the suffering of newborns in limbo. I will draw a lesson from it in every medical emergency situation where the humanization of practices can help us out of a difficulty. Any place where the choice between living and dying is at play—the intensive care unit, for example—can benefit from the addition of psychoanalytic help. It is not a question of assisting the dying, but of sometimes helping to identify what, in the act of letting oneself die, may lie on the unconscious register.

One of my patients had me summoned to the hospital where he had just had surgery following a myocardial infarction. He was in a profound state of depression, which made him want to die even though the surgery seemed to be a great success. He understood, after speaking to me, that there might be reasons for his depression that he had not suspected at first. Although he said he wanted to die, that desire was not his own, but rather the effect of a different unconscious wish. If he let himself die, it would be to conform to his mother's hatred of him, which he expressed, in astonishingly condensed form, as follows: "Given her august age, I see only one explanation for her longevity: What keeps her alive is the fact that she hasn't seen me dead yet!"

The reason for that blunt remark, heavy with implications related to his family history—his unsevered connection to imaginary issues, which left his life hanging by the thread of his mother's desire, and his resulting failure to accede to the symbolic, which made him turn toward death because he was never truly "born"—is beyond the scope of this book. But my patient regained his freedom to live. This is an opportunity for me to say that, in medically serious or even desperate cases, psychoanalytic listening can have its importance.

Its effect is on the same order as that in force for newborns: to restore to them their words, access to their history, and the ability to choose between the death drive gnawing away at them and the desire for life they discover within themselves. That is the lesson for humanity that babies teach us. Thereby, they show us the horizon of the psychoanalyst's work: Allow each one to be constantly born and reborn to life, in accordance with each one's desire.

Acknowledgments

After working with and thinking about children of preverbal age for many years, I was able to work as a psychoanalyst with newborns in a maternity ward. That very special clinic gradually produced in me a desire to bear witness. The originality of the approach and the effects I was able to observe have continued to raise questions for me and to orient my research in various directions; they have made me open to every multidisciplinary approach.

My thanks to René Frydman and the entire staff on the Béclère maternity ward for their confidence and for the quality of our collaboration.

Thanks as well to Lucien Kokh, for his lessons and conceptual suggestions, which allowed me to establish the foundations of my practice.

The psychoanalyst Hervé Bernard decided to work with me on a long-term basis. He followed me to the maternity ward, listened to me, and collaborated with me, placing his writing talents and his education at the service of this book. My thanks to him for the depth and sensitivity of our work together.

To Mary Shepherd and the American psychoanalysts who trust my work.

Notes

INTRODUCTION: "WE HEREBY ANNOUNCE ..."

1   J. Lacan, "Le temps logique et l'assertion de certitude anticipée,"
     [Logical time and the assertion of anticipated certainty] in *Ecrits*
     (Paris: Seuil, 1966), 197–203.

1. THE INTERESTS OF THE BABY

1   Françoise Dolto's extensive bibliography attests to her contribution
     to psychoanalysis. It is well known that she had no penchant for
     brevity, and the problem for readers is to find their bearings in a body
     of work marked by a profusion of clinical notes. I find that one of the
     most successful books, which allows us to understand the novelty and
     theoretical coherence of her works, is Gérard Guillerault's *Le corps
     psychique* (Ed. universitaires, 1989). To date, this book has not been
     translated into English.
2   See, in particular, Charpak et al., "Rey-Martinez Kangaroo Mother
     Program: An Alternative Way of Caring for Low Birth Weight
     Infants?" in *Pediatrics* 14, no. 6 (December 1994): 804–10.
3   See Daniel Stern, *The Interpersonal World of the Infant* (New York:
     Basic Books, 1985).
4   Denis Vasse, *L'ombilic et la voix* (Paris: Seuil, 1974), 18.
5   Françoise Dolto, *L'image inconsciente du corps* (Paris: Seuil, 1984),
     47–48.

2. A CHILD IS BORN AT LEAST TWICE

1 S. Freud, *Three Essays on the Theory of Sexuality,* in *The Standard Edition of the Complete Psychological Works of Sigmund Freud,* vol. 7, trans. James Strachey (New York: Basic Books, 1962).

2 Ibid., 191.

3 S. Freud, "Pour introduire la discussion sur l'onanisme," in *Résultats, idées, problèmes* (PUF, 1984), 1:183 [This passage does not appear in English translations of Freud's works. I have therefore translated from the French edition—*trans.*]. See also S. Freud, "On the Sexual Theories of Children," in *Standard Edition of the Complete Psychological Works,* 9:205–26.

4 For Winnicott, "primary maternal preoccupation" designates the mother's increased sensitivity in the late stages of pregnancy and after birth. That acute, even "abnormal" degree of adaptation to the baby's needs declines little by little as the mother stops identifying so entirely with her baby, gradually allowing the child to differentiate the mother from his "self." See D. Winnicott, *Through Pediatrics to Psychoanalysis* (New York: Basic Books, 1975).

5 On this subject, see M. C. Busnel and F. Morel, *Le langage des bébés,* ed. Jacques Grancher (Paris, 1993), esp. F. Morel's evidence in "Ecoute, mon bébé, c'est ta maman," 96–98; and M. Couronne, "Le prématuré, un bébé à part entière," 130–38. See also J. P. Lecanuet, C. Granier-Deferre, and M. C. Busnel, "Sensorialité foetale, Ontogenèse des systèmes sensoriels, conséquences de leur fonctionnement foetal," in *Médecine péri-natale I* (Paris, 1989), 201–25.

6 There is an enormous scientific bibliography on this subject. See, among the most recent publications, J. P. Lecanuet, "L'expérience auditive prénatale," and C. Fassbender, "La sensibilité auditive du nourrisson aux paramètres acoustiques du langage et de la musique," in *Naissance et développement du sens musical,* ed. I. Deliège and J. A. Sloboda (PUF, 1995), 7–38 and 63–99; J. Mehler et al., "Discrimination de la langue maternelle par le nouveau-né," in *C. R. Acad. des Sciences de Paris,* series 3, vol. 303, no. 15 (1986); M. C. Busnel, "Pre- and Perinatal Audition and the Relationship between Mother and Child," *Annals of the New York Academy of Sciences* (New York, 1992); and "Is There Prenatal Culture?" in Gardner et al., *The Ethological Roots of the Culture* (Dordrecht, Netherlands: Kluwer Acad. Publishing, 1994), 285–314.

7 L. A. Petitto, P. F. Marentette, "Babbling in the Manual Mode: Evidence for the Ontogeny of Language," *Science* 251 (March 1991): 1493–96.

8   Konrad Lorenz, the founder of modern ethology, theorized this with
    animals; the psychoanalyst René Spitz evoked it regarding institu-
    tionalized children; Françoise Dolto put it into practice during the
    Second World War; and Benoit Schaal proved it experimentally in
    the late 1980s.
9   Dolto, *L'image inconsciente du corps,* 212–13.
10 S. Kierkegaard, *Repetition: An Essay in Experimental Psychology,* trans.
    Walter Lowrie (Princeton: Princeton University Press, 1946), 44
    [translation modified—*trans.*].
11 C. Simon, *Le vent* (Ed. de Minuit, 1975).
12 B. Cyrulnik, *Les nourritures affectives* (Ed. Odile Jacob, 1993), 59ff.
13 Her methodology and results are described in her first book, A. Pion-
    telli, *From Fetus to Child—An Observational and Psychoanalytic Study*
    (New York: Routledge, 1992).
14 M. Szejer, R. Stewart, *Ces neuf mois-là* (Robert Laffont, 1994, 2003).
15 I am greatly indebted, for the reflections that follow, to C. Dolto,
    who was the first to defend and demonstrate haptonomy in France.
    Those wishing to better understand haptonomy may refer to her arti-
    cles, "Haptonomie pré- and postnatale," *Journal de Pédiatrie et de
    Puériculture,* no. 1 (1991): 36–46; "Génération, espoir et souffrance,"
    in *Actes du Colloque "Souffrances, quel sens aujourd'hui?"* (Erès, 1992),
    111–12. See also Frans Veldman, *Haptonomie—Science de l'affectivité*
    (PUF, 1989).
16 Marie Thirion, *Les compétences du nouveau-né* (Ramsay, 1986).

3. SPEECH, LANGUAGE, AND
   MEMORY IN THE NEWBORN

1   Dolto, *L'image inconsciente du corps,* 213.
2   F. Dolto, *Séminaire de psychanalyse d'enfants* (Seuil, coll. "Points es-
    sais"), 2:174ff.
3   M. C. Busnel, comments at the fourth Salon International Psychia-
    trie et Système Nerveux Central, Paris, 19 October 1996.
4   A. R. Damasio, *L'erreur de Descartes—La raison des émotions* (Ed.
    Odile Jacob, 1995).
5   G. M. Edelman, *The Remembered Present: A Biological Theory of Con-
    sciousness* (New York: Basic Books, 1989). See, in particular, chapter
    12, "The Conscious and the Unconscious," and the epilogue.
6   Lacan, "Le temps logique," 891.
7   B. Cyrulnik, *La naissance du sens* (Hachette, 1991).
8   Ibid., 57ff.
9   Ibid., 55.

10   G. Gelbert, *Lire, c'est vivre* (Ed. Odile Jacob, 1994).

11   P. Valéry, *Tel quel* (Gallimard, "Pléiade"), 497.

12   D. Stern, *The Interpersonal World of the Infant* (New York: Basic Books, 1985), 177.

13   On the baby's relation to her mother during breastfeeding, see A. Naouri, "La bouche et le voeu tu," in *Revue de Médecine Psychosomatique* (September 1987).

14   I. Rosenfield, *The Invention of Memory* (New York: Basic Books, 1988).

15   Ibid., 193.

16   B. Cyrulnik, *Les nourritures affectives* (Ed. Odile Jacob, 1993), 61.

17   J. P. Tassin, "Peut-on trouver un lien entre l'inconscient psychanalytique et les connaissances actuelles en neuro-biologie?" in *Neuro-Psy* 4, no. 8 (1989): 421–34; idem, "Schizophrénie et neuro-transmission: Un excès de traitement analogique?" in *L'Encéphale* (1996), supplement 3, 91–98.

18   P. Quignard, *Le nom sur le bout de la langue* (POL ed., 1993).

4. DOING PSYCHOANALYSIS ON A MATERNITY WARD

1   D. Vasse, *Se tenir debout et marcher* (Gallimard, coll. "Sur le champ," 1995), 248.

5. FROM BIRTH TO LIFE'S LIMBO

1   F. Dolto, *Séminaire de psychanalyse d'enfants* (Seuil, coll. "Points,"), 1:170.

2   Dolto, *Séminaire de psychanalyse d'enfants,* 1:114ff.

3   A. Didier-Weill, *Les trois temps de la loi* (Seuil, 1995).

4   F. Dolto, *Dialogues québecois,* 71–72.

5   M. Thirion, *Les compétences du nouveau-né,* 37.

6   R. Frydman, *L'irrésistible désir de naissance* (PUF, 1986), 41.

6. CONFIDENTIAL CHILDBIRTH

1   Dolto, *Séminaire de psychanalyse d'enfants,* 2:98–99.

2   Since January 2002, French law concerning confidential childbirth has been modified. An organization, CNAOP (Counseil National pour l'Accès aux Origines Personelles, [National Council for Access to Personal Information on One's Origins]) has been founded, with the express purpose of managing the identities of children born confidentially. When a woman gives birth anonymously, she can

deposit her identity, address, and elements of the history of the child with the CNAOP, and these elements will be held in secret. If the adopted child later wants to know more about his birth parents, he can ask the CNAOP to search for them. Then, if the birth parents agree, the CNAOP helps the child and the parents meet. This can happen only if the child makes the initial request. A child is never contacted by a birth parent if he did not ask first. But the parents can contact CNAOP anytime to tell them they don't want their identities to be held secret anymore and that if the child appears, they want to be reached. This helps some women (and men) who, after a certain period of time, change their minds and wish to see the child they abandoned at birth.

3   Y. Knibiehler, "Désir d'enfant," in *Etudes Freudiennes,* no. 32 (November 1991): 143–57.

4   F. Héritier, *Masculin/Féminin* (Ed. Odile Jacob, 1996).

5   U. Eco, *L'île du jour d'avant* (Grasset, 1996), 420.

EPILOGUE: THE CHOICE TO LIVE

1   J. Lacan, "Le temps logique," 197–213.

Index

abandonment, 189, 209. *See also* confidential childbirth

abortion: and confidential childbirth, 203; late-term abortion of deformed twin, 37–39; mother's consideration of, 63, 64

acknowledgment of birth of child, 225–27

adoption: baby blues for adoptive mothers, 146–47; and family secrets of adopted child, 215–16; in French Polynesia and Tahiti, 217–18; laws on, 18; and pain of early separation for child, 33–35; psychoanalytic work with adopted children, 24. *See also* confidential childbirth

Africa, 143–44, 179, 195

alcoholism, 4, 8, 208

amenorrhea, 3, 5–6

amnesia. *See* infantile amnesia

amniocentesis, 164

analogical processing, 113, 114–15, 117

anorexia of mother, 47–48

Antinori, Severino, 136

Antoine Béclère Hospital maternity ward, 13, 25–30, 36–37. *See also* hospital staff

Antony state nursery, 13, 21, 24, 25, 129, 190, 198

anxiety of fathers, 92–93

anxiety of mothers, 2–5, 7–8, 93, 99. *See also* baby blues

Arab women, 219–20. *See also* Muslims

Ariès, Philippe, 16

asthma, 233

attachment, 79–80, 188

attracting fields of memory, 113–14

automatism of repetition, 66–67

babbling, 97, 98; with hands, 55–56

babies: and confusion between need and desire, 160; continuity from fetus to infant, 68–74; Freud on onanism of, 46; hand babbling by, 55–56; mortality rate for, 17–18; personality of, 167; societal interest in and care for, 16–19. *See also* newborns; premature babies; psychoanalysis with newborns; twins

baby blues: and adoptive mothers,

Kierkegaard, Sören, 67
Klein, Melanie, 47
Knibiehler, Yvonne, 223
Kokh, Lucien, 61, 62, 134, 159–60

Lacan, Jacques, 11–12, 44, 96, 159
lactation, 36, 106, 108, 148
language: creativity in, 95–96; and
    dream of woman with cancer,
    83–84; "hole of language," 68,
    117–18, 144, 159; and language
    bath, 74, 100–101, 159; and
    mother tongue, 54–55, 102;
    newborn's aptitude for, 93–
    103; newborn's recognition of
    mother's language, 54–55, 82–
    83; newborn's understanding
    of, 81, 82–83, 84, 102–3; potential
    space of language, 159–60; and
    semantics of newborn, 84–86;
    and syllable formation, 101–3;
    written versus oral language,
    170. See also sign language;
    speech; voice
language bath, 74, 100–101, 159
language delays and defects, 170
laws: on acknowledgment of child
    following birth, 225–27; on adop-
    tion, 18; on confidential child-
    birth, 18, 189–91, 205, 206,
    213–14, 216, 218–19
Lebovici, Serge, 90, 161–62
LeBoyer, Frederick, 153–54
limbic system, 87, 94, 110
limbo: and baby blues, 14–15,
    139–40, 159–68, 169, 170–71,
    222–24; and confidential birth,
    139–40, 222–24; correspondence
    between days following concep-
    tion and, 234; definition of, 14,
    223; etymology of word, 223; and
    psychoanalysis with newborns,

230–32, 234–36; and symbolic
    birth, 139–41, 168–71, 234–35
listening: to mothers after child-
    birth, 35–37; in psychoanalysis
    with newborns, 10–11, 35–43,
    128–29; psychoanalytic concep-
    tion of, 25. See also psychoanaly-
    sis; psychoanalysis with
    newborns
living probes, 134
Luria, Alexander, 115

Malraux, André, 63
Marr, David, 109
maternal identification, 6–7, 107,
    152, 171–73
maternal instinct, 221. See also
    mothers
maternity ward. See Antoine Béclère
    Hospital maternity ward
meaning of life for newborns, 47–50
mediation function of hospital staff,
    132–38
medically assisted conception. See
    reproductive technologies
melancholic depression, 142–43
memory: attracting fields of, 113–
    14; creative memory, 104–8; and
    dreams, 109–10, 112–13; and emo-
    tion, 87; and extracting and slow-
    ing down information, 114–15;
    and infantile amnesia, 70, 91,
    115–18; neurobiology of, 86–87;
    of newborns, 103–18; and perma-
    nence of self, 103–4; process of
    memorization, 108–18; research
    on, 108–12; and role of psychoan-
    alyst working with newborns,
    117–18; screen memories, 115;
    Stern on, 103–4
menstrual period. See amenorrhea
metaphors, 80, 96, 97, 158

37–39; mother as twin, 63–65; mother of, 63–65; mourning by child for dead twin, 40–42, 104–5; movement of, 72–73; Piontelli's study of, 70–73, 104. *See also* triplets

umbilical castration, 168, 170–71, 178, 181, 182
umbilical cord: attempts to reestablish connection with, in infants' respiratory problems, 177, 210; cutting of, 33, 160, 168
unconscious, 103, 114, 185
University of Turin, 70
urination by baby, 2–5, 7–8

Valéry, Paul, 103
Vasse, Denis, 32–33, 123
Velman, Frans, 74n
vision. *See* gaze
visual anosognosia, 94
visual cortex, 94

voice: baby's search for mother's voice, 57–58; ducks and voice recognition, 86; fetus's recognition of mother's voice, 54, 74; first wail of newborns, 33; newborn's recognition of parents' voices, 33, 52, 54–56, 57, 76–77; and premature babies, 52–53; prosodic elements of speech, 82; in psychoanalysis with newborns, 31–35; and "word holes," 68, 117–18, 144, 159. *See also* language; speech

weight gain in newborns, 92–93
weight loss in newborns. *See* eating problems of newborns
Winnicott, Donald, 47, 51, 103
withdrawal psychosis, 142–43
"word holes," 68, 117–18, 144, 159
written versus oral language, 170

Yugoslavia, 215